Simply Eliot

Simply Eliot

JOSEPH MADDREY

SIMPLY CHARLY
NEW YORK

Cover Illustration by José Ramos
Cover Design by Scarlett Rugers

permissions@simplycharly.com

ISBN: 978-1-943657-25-4

Brought to you by http://simplycharly.com

For Jewel Spears Brooker, who encouraged me to write this book.

Contents

Praise for *Simply Eliot*

"The next time I teach Eliot to undergrads I will assign this swift, witty, enjoyable invitation to T. S. Eliot's work and thought. Maddrey knows everything about Eliot, but he grinds no axe which frees professors and students to grind their own. Scrupulously footnoted for professional use, not short but concise, it is stuffed with unfamiliar and apt quotations. Maddrey quotes a 1949 interview about *The Cocktail Party*, in which Eliot said, 'If there is nothing more in the play than what I was aware of meaning, then it must be a pretty thin piece of work.' There's the New Criticism in 25 words, 21 of them monosyllables. Eliot asks us to quit asking what he thought and to do some thinking ourselves. This book will help."

–George J. Leonard, author of *Into the Light of Things* and *The End of Innocence*. Professor of Interdisciplinary Humanities, San Francisco State University

"Joseph Maddrey provides an illuminating spiritual biography of T. S. Eliot that treats his writings as markers of Eliot's lifelong spiritual drama and development while avoiding reducing his poetry to biography because he treats the texts as products of creation that all can contemplate. Maddrey admiringly captures the creativity of both Eliot's character and his poetry. The two are elusive not only because Eliot's poetry employs a vast and encyclopedic storehouse of poetic images ('3,000 years of word made flesh'), but also because his poetry strives to move 'beyond poetry,' at the apophatic 'ever-present frontier of consciousness–where words fail, though meanings persist.' Maddrey introduces Eliot to a new generation of readers, and guides wanderers anew at the 'point of intersection with the timeless / With time.'"

–John von Heyking, Professor of Political Science at the University of Lethbridge, Alberta, Canada

"T. S. Eliot considered that 'a worthwhile biography should show the development of an artist and give readers a proper sense of how each work of art fits within the whole.' In *Simply Eliot* Joseph Maddrey has fulfilled the directive, brilliantly compressing a gargantuan amount of previous Eliot studies and providing a fresh dynamic manual for understanding this storied literary icon."

–Quinton Hallett, Poet, and Author of *Mrs. Schrödinger's Breast*

"*Simply Eliot* is an accessible, artfully-written book that positions a well-known literary figure in a seemingly new landscape. One of the book's greatest strengths is its extensive engagement with archival sources. Maddrey draws on those sources to give weight and depth to his narrative, which weaves interpretations–close-readings, even–of Eliot's poetry into the broad strokes of his biography and intellectual genealogy. The approach is neither reductive nor esoteric, and Maddrey's way with language draws the reader–one suddenly realizes one is reading and enjoying literary criticism. For this reason, the book will appeal not just to an audience of academics or students, but to intelligent, cultured people of all kinds."

–Dr. Siân White, Associate Professor of English, James Madison University

"Joseph Maddrey's *Simply Eliot* is an elegant addition to the Great Lives series, providing an authoritative introduction to T. S. Eliot's work and influences. Accessible and yet well researched, Maddrey's biography gives readers a deeper understanding and appreciation for Eliot's life and his development as an artist by tracing the personal and critical influences of the individual poems and plays written throughout the writer's long career. Maddrey focuses on the individual works themselves to demonstrate how each fits into the whole and represents Eliot's journey as a spiritual seeker and artist. Maddrey's book will make a great introduction to all who are interested in Eliot, as well as to everyone and anyone who wants to learn more. *Simply Eliot* is simply what all biographies should be."

–Carol Scarvalone Kushner, Professor of English & Humanities at Dutchess Community College

"Joseph Maddrey's brief vita of Eliot is a tale of a search for identities both human and divine. Maddrey is right to say that 'Eliot's total commitment to the church transformed his poetry.' Was that church, though, the Church of England, with its distinctive patrimony of the King James Bible, and Lancelot Andrewes, and George Herbert, and their like, or the Anglican faith as a world religion which Eliot experienced first in the USA during his flight from Unitarianism? Maddrey's analysis of Eliot as an American High-Church Anglican living in Britain insightfully explores the relationship between religious and cultural identities, and helpfully places Eliot, nationally and religiously respectively, as 'stranger and pilgrim.'"

–The Reverend Graeme Napier MA MPhil (Oxon), Rector, St. John's in the Village, Greenwich Village, New York

"This relatively brief account of the life of T. S. Eliot admirably enlarges one's appreciation of his poetry and other writings by situating them within their historical, cultural, and religious backgrounds. Not of least value is the final section entitled 'Suggested Reading', which is actually a summary of the responses of critical scholarship to Eliot's work rather a mere list of books."

–The Revd Dr. Paul Bradshaw, Professor Emeritus of Liturgical Studies, University of Notre Dame

"I had to stop my daily life, almost, to read *Simply Eliot*; for me, it is compelling, refreshing, and genuinely exciting to read a biography that speaks to Virginia Woolf's 'common reader.' *Cats* saved Eliot for millions of people, but it did not make people want to read Eliot's challenging poetry. I think Maddrey's book will."

–Charles W. Spurgeon, Professor Emeritus at Marymount University and author of *The Poetry of Westminster Abbey* and *J. Henry Shorthouse, The Author of John Inglesant (with Reference to T. S. Eliot and C. G. Jung)*

Other *Great Lives*

Simply Austen by Joan Klingel Ray
Simply Beckett by Katherine Weiss
Simply Beethoven by Leon Plantinga
Simply Chekhov by Carol Apollonio
Simply Chomsky by Raphael Salkie
Simply Chopin by William Smialek
Simply Darwin by Michael Ruse
Simply Descartes by Kurt Smith
Simply Dickens by Paul Schlicke
Simply Dirac by Helge Kragh
Simply Einstein by Jimena Canales
Simply Euler by Robert E. Bradley
Simply Faulkner by Philip Weinstein
Simply Fitzgerald by Kim Moreland
Simply Freud by Stephen Frosh
Simply Gödel by Richard Tieszen
Simply Hegel by Robert L. Wicks
Simply Hitchcock by David Sterritt
Simply Joyce by Margot Norris
Simply Machiavelli by Robert Fredona
Simply Napoleon by J. David Markham & Matthew Zarzeczny
Simply Nietzsche by Peter Kail
Simply Proust by Jack Jordan
Simply Riemann by Jeremy Gray
Simply Sartre by David Detmer
Simply Tolstoy by Donna Tussing Orwin
Simply Stravinsky by Pieter van den Toorn
Simply Turing by Michael Olinick
Simply Wagner by Thomas S. Grey
Simply Wittgenstein by James C. Klagge

Series Editor's Foreword

Simply Charly's "Great Lives" series offers brief but authoritative introductions to the world's most influential people–scientists, artists, writers, economists, and other historical figures whose contributions have had a meaningful and enduring impact on our society.

Each book provides an illuminating look at the works, ideas, personal lives, and the legacies these individuals left behind, also shedding light on the thought processes, specific events, and experiences that led these remarkable people to their groundbreaking discoveries or other achievements. Additionally, every volume explores various challenges they had to face and overcome to make history in their respective fields, as well as the little-known character traits, quirks, strengths, and frailties, myths, and controversies that sometimes surrounded these personalities.

Our authors are prominent scholars and other top experts who have dedicated their careers to exploring each facet of their subjects' work and personal lives.

Unlike many other works that are merely descriptions of the major milestones in a person's life, the "Great Lives" series goes above and beyond the standard format and content. It brings substance, depth, and clarity to the sometimes-complex lives and works of history's most powerful and influential people.

We hope that by exploring this series, readers will not only gain new knowledge and understanding of what drove these geniuses, but also find inspiration for their own lives. Isn't this what a great book is supposed to do?

Charles Carlini, Simply Charly
New York City

Preface

There is nothing simple about T. S. Eliot. At least, that's the simple conclusion to be drawn from the existence of thousands of books, essays, and dissertations about the Nobel Prize-winning poet. Collectively, this body of critical work has created a popular conception of Eliot as an impossibly complex writer and a man of many contradictory masks. Critics have presented him as an avant-garde poet and conservative critic, a modernist and a traditionalist, a Romantic and a Classicist, a philosopher and a moralist, an American and a European, a proto-fascist and a pseudo-mystic, a bigot and a sage. Each of these masks can be peeled away, but then what are we left with? Who was T. S. Eliot and what did he really stand for?

First and foremost, he is the author of several very influential poems, including "The Love Song of J. Alfred Prufrock," *The Waste Land*, *The Hollow Men*, *Ash-Wednesday*, and *Four Quartets*. Even those who have never read these poems have probably encountered some key phrases from them—enigmatic allusions to measuring out one's life with coffee spoons, or enduring the cruelty of April, or watching the world end with a whimper instead of a bang. Those who are familiar with Eliot's poetry may have an impression of him as an esoteric wordsmith who captured the world-weary "spirit of the age" in post-WWI Europe, or as a religious conservative who championed Christianity as the solution to all the problems of the modern world. Both are oversimplifications.

In academic circles, Eliot is usually remembered as an influential literary critic who coined several memorable phrases, including "objective correlative," "mythical method," and "auditory imagination." His breakthrough essay, "Tradition and the Individual Talent," provided a loose basis for New Criticism, a movement in literary theory prevalent in American universities during the middle of the 20th century. Other major essays and lectures revolutionized the study of metaphysical poetry and revitalized interest in 17th-century English poets like John Donne, contextualizing their work as part of a broader literary tradition from the 14th-century Italian poet Dante Alighieri to the 19th-century French poet Charles Baudelaire. For several years, Eliot tried to clarify the distinction between literary Classicism and Romanticism, before reframing the dichotomy in terms of orthodoxy vs. heresy, and turning his focus toward social criticism. In his later years, he suggested that his critical work would endure mainly as an aid to understanding his own development as a poet. That is how many scholars (and the author of this book) choose to use it.

Eliot's work as a playwright has receded further into the background in recent years, but a new generation of scholars recognizes that his early verse dramas—especially *Sweeney Agonistes: Fragments of an Aristophanic Melodrama*, *Murder in the Cathedral*, and *The Family Reunion*—are vital to understanding the poet's body of work. Toward the end of his life, Eliot all but abandoned verse poetry in favor of stage plays. He achieved his greatest commercial success with the contemporary comedies *The Cocktail Party*, *The Confidential Clerk*, and *The Elder Statesman*, and those works subtly embody his ultimate truths.

Although Eliot once famously declared that critics should never concern themselves with the personal details of an artist's life, critics and biographers have often been tempted to mine the specifics of his personal life for insights into his body of work. At times, the poet took the same approach to studying writers who preceded him. In 1937, he characterized the collected essays of his late friend Paul Elmer More as a chronicle of More's "spiritual pilgrimage."[1] He also wrote that More's journey was an "auxiliary" to his own.[2] Like Eliot, More was born in St. Louis and educated at Harvard under the tutelage of Irving Babbitt, and he extensively studied Eastern religion and Western philosophy before turning away from his Unitarian upbringing and embracing the Anglican form of Christianity. What was important to Eliot—about his own work, and More's—was not the destination, but the journey. By studying Eliot's poetry and plays within the context of the author's life, we can better understand him and his lifelong search for an intellectually coherent and authentically-felt worldview, and better assess his importance as a literary figure and a cultural icon.

Of course, it's difficult to trace that journey without contemplating some of the more intimate details of the poet's life—and here we run the risk of getting mired in celebrity gossip that may or may not illuminate his work. Critics and biographers have thoroughly examined Eliot's troubled relationship with his first wife, Vivienne Haigh-Wood, who was committed to a mental hospital in 1938. Some of these studies have depicted the poet as emotionally abusive, even misogynistic. Eliot's friendship (in the years 1910 through 1915) with a Frenchman named Jean Verdenal has also been a subject of much scrutiny, and the basis for some spurious claims about Eliot's sexual orientation. The poet's cohabitation with the English scholar John Hayward (from 1946 until early 1957) and his marriage to his much younger secretary Valerie Fletcher have also prompted speculation. Hidden behind all these relationships is Eliot's decades-long friendship with Emily Hale, the reputed lady-in-waiting who hoped to be his second wife. The details of that relationship will be illuminated more fully in 2020 when approximately 1,131 letters from the poet to Hale become available to researchers at Princeton University. Until then, critics (and novelists) will continue to hazard guesses about the "truth" of Eliot's romantic and sexual life.

To be fair, Eliot himself once suggested in a private letter that an author's sexual life is worthy of studying if that author is "a spiritual type, *not* a mere abnormal."[3] We can safely assume that Eliot regarded himself as a spiritual type, but we can also understand why the poet—or *anyone*—would want to maintain their privacy about the most intimate details of their life. In 1927, Eliot wrote to his mother that if a biography was ever written about him, he hoped it wouldn't include any private details. When the poet died in 1965, and for many years afterward, his widow Valerie followed the poet's strict instructions not to sanction an official biography. As a result, there has never been a definitive biography, and countless writers (including several of the poet's friends and peers) have attempted to fill that void–with varying degrees of sympathy and accuracy.

In 2009, after witnessing many years of armchair criticism, Valerie Eliot announced the commencement of a massive editorial project to publish all of the poet's work–including countless previously unpublished essays and letters–in scholarly editions. Today, as these editions become available, it is possible once again to see Eliot himself through the dense fog of secondary studies. Readers can now directly appeal to the poet for all the answers he is able and willing to give about himself and his work. The material in these editions also provides humanizing details about the man heretofore known as "the invisible poet." Among other things, Eliot was a lover of cheese, cats, whiskey, and detective stories; a hater of heights and cows; and the proud inventor of the word "bullshit."

In a few short years, a wealth of publications has produced new answers to old questions, including this one: *What sort of biography might have pleased* T. S. *Eliot?* In 1918, in one of his earliest book reviews, the poet wrote that "the biographer ought to know a good deal about the art of his subject, if the subject is an artist; but his main purpose is to present facts and to deal with his subject's attitude toward his art."[4] In 1961, in one of his last major essays, he offered a personal note about the importance of accurately contextualizing such information: "I find myself constantly irritated by having my words, perhaps written thirty or forty years ago, quoted as if I had uttered them yesterday [...] Rare is the writer who, quoting me, says 'this is what Mr. Eliot thought (or felt) in 1933.'"[5] So in Eliot's view, a worthwhile biography should show the *development* of an artist, and give readers a proper sense of how each work of art fits within the whole.

For Eliot, an artist's creative work–the whole of his creative work, not merely the "major" work–was the only true biography. Eliot covertly recommended to potential biographers a holistic reading of his own work when he wrote of Shakespeare's oeuvre as a single poem. The whole of an artist's work, he asserted, gives "the pattern, or we may say the undertone, of the personal emotion, the personal drama and struggle, which no biography, however full and intimate could give us."[6]

This statement has done little to deter biographers or critics, the best of whom continue to indulge their own enthusiasm for particular artists and works of art—just as Eliot himself did. The poet realized that his own literary criticism was strongest when he was writing about work that he personally enjoyed and admired. Genuine enjoyment and appreciation prompt us—as readers and critics—to explore endlessly, in order to better understand and better appreciate art. This is our beginning.

Joseph Maddrey
Los Angeles, CA

1. Prufrock and Other Observations

An American Childhood

In his 1948 book *Notes towards the Definition of Culture*, T. S. Eliot wrote, "The primary channel of transmission of culture is the family: no man wholly escapes from the kind, or wholly surpasses the degree, of culture which he acquired from his early environment."[1] Accordingly, Eliot himself never wholly escaped his identity as an American and, even more so, as a member of a proud and prosperous family with strong roots in colonial New England and the Midwest. He openly acknowledged in a 1959 interview that his poetry "in its emotional springs [...] comes from America."[2]

Thomas Stearns Eliot was born in St. Louis, Missouri, on September 26, 1888, the youngest of six children–five sisters, born between 1869 and 1877, and one brother, born in 1879. His father, Henry Ware Eliot (1843–1919), was a pragmatic businessman, and a deeply committed Unitarian. Family members recalled him as "a Christian gentleman of charm and humor" and "a man of sensibility who could erect defenses and keep his thoughts to himself."[3] According to his niece Abigail, Henry was also "almost stone-deaf," which may have contributed to poor communication between him and his youngest child.[4] Indeed, young Tom seems to have had a distant relationship with his father. There is perhaps an echo of the relationship in Eliot's late play, *The Confidential Clerk* when Sir Claude remembers his father: "I never understood him. / I was too young. And when I was mature enough / To understand him, he was not there."[5]

Tom had a more intimate relationship with his mother, Charlotte Champe Stearns (1843–1929), a schoolteacher and amateur religious poet. She was the first person to champion him as a writer, and was his closest companion for many years. Eliot's youngest sibling, his only brother Henry Jr., was nine years older, and the family lived in a run-down neighborhood where few other children resided. In 1905, Charlotte wrote to Eliot's prep school headmaster that she was concerned about her son's lack of friends his own age, and about her own habit of talking to him as if he was an adult, rather than treating him as a child. Combining this statement with certain details about his physical limitations and the inheritance of an anxious, nervous temperament, one gets a sense of young Tom as an introvert and a bit of a mama's boy. His sense of isolation drew him toward escapist literature. Tom's cousin Eleanor remembered, "He could sit all day in his little rocking chair. And he'd read anything. [His mother] never supervised his reading." Cousin Abigail added, "He was thoughtful. Bright, of course. Very bright. Reserved. Mischievous, but rather overwhelmed at that time by his family."[6]

Eliot's parents both came from proud middle-class families with very particular ideas about life. From young Tom's perspective, the patriarch of his clan was his paternal grandfather William Greenleaf Eliot (1811–1887). At age 55, Eliot remembered, "I was brought up to be very much aware of him: so much so that as a child I thought of him as still head of the family—a ruler for whom *in absentia* my grandmother stood as vice regent."[7] As a young man, William Greenleaf Eliot had moved from his ancestral New England home to the frontier city of St. Louis, where he devoted himself to public service and founded Washington University and the first Unitarian Church west of the Mississippi River. Tom was raised in that church, and later remembered that its moral instructions were imparted in terms of black-or-white. He elaborated (according to his friend William Turner Levy), "All that concerned my family was 'right or wrong,' what was 'done and not done.'"[8] He might have specified that these were the concerns of his immediate family, the most recent generations of Eliots. In contrast, the poet felt that he had inherited the acute sense of sin known to his Puritan ancestors, including Andrew Eliot, a guilt-ridden participant in the Salem Witch Trials.

Tom once wrote the following note to himself (on the back of an envelope), "You either believe in the reality of *sin* or you don't—*that* is the important moral distinction—not whether you are good or bad."[9] In 1955, he characterized himself as a man with "a Catholic cast of mind, a Calvinistic heritage, and a Puritanical temperament."[10] The sense of sin haunted his life like a ghost in a Nathaniel Hawthorne story.

During these early years, other influences were equally significant. From the beginning, Tom's sense of place was powerful. He internalized bleak impressions of the now-rundown industrial neighborhood his grandfather had settled: yellow smoke and fog, half-deserted streets and old women gathering firewood from vacant lots. Later, when he encountered comparably unsavory landscapes in Boston and London, and in the works of certain French and English poets, he would equate them with these memories and incorporate them into his poetry.

In contrast with these sordid images, Eliot also vividly remembered the rapturous but ghostly sound of children laughing and playing next to his childhood home. A high brick wall marked the boundary between the Eliot family's backyard garden and The Mary Institute, an all-girls' school founded by his grandfather and named for an aunt who had died in infancy. The poet remembered one day when he ventured beyond the wall and encountered a group of young girls staring back at him. Terrified, he turned and ran. The experience enhanced his feelings of isolation.

The lush environs of the Mississippi River made perhaps the most indelible impression on the future poet. A close friend described how, as a boy, Eliot "could hear its flow as he lay in bed at night or as he sat with his family under the gaslight in the window recess, smelling the grapes in autumn and the delicate keen scent of the April ailanthus in the yard which opened onto the girls' school beside his home."[11] Eliot himself remembered the majesty of the river during flood-time, and asserted that "there is something in having passed one's childhood beside the big river, which is incommunicable to those who have not."[12] In *Four Quartets*, he would describe the Mississippi River as "a strong brown god," suggesting that he may have had a personal experience of what the erstwhile Unitarian poet Ralph Waldo Emerson called "God or Nature."

For all of its influence, St. Louis comprised only half of what Eliot would call (in the poem *Burnt Norton*) his "first world." From the time when he was six years old, the Eliot family spent summers near Gloucester, Massachusetts, where young Tom took up sailing and explored the coastline to the north. He and his brother Henry fell in love with romantic tales of the courageous local fishermen, and (mistakenly) imagined themselves the heirs of a sailor who was shipwrecked there in 1635. The younger brother developed such a strong affinity for this natural environment that he eventually felt conflicted about his own origins. When the poet was in his 40s, he recalled that as a child he felt like a nomad, because he was emotionally torn between his family's New England heritage and his own experience of life in Missouri. In 1928, he wrote that both places filled him with a sense of longing: "In New England I missed the long dark river, the ailanthus trees, the flaming cardinal birds, the high limestone bluffs where we searched for fossil shell-fish; in Missouri I missed the fir trees, the bay and goldenrod, the song-sparrows, the red granite and the blue sea of Massachusetts."[13] Especially the sea. According to biographer Peter Ackroyd, at one time Eliot planned to write a book of childhood reminiscences entitled *The River and the Sea*. Instead, the river and the sea finally merged in *Four Quartets*.

All of these early impressions–"snapshots" representing "the depths of feeling into which we cannot peer"–helped to awaken the poet in T. S. Eliot.[14] His appreciation for formal poetry may have begun with the discovery of Edwin Arnold's *The Light of Asia*, which he read enthusiastically and repeatedly as a child, or with *The Collected Works of Edgar Allan Poe*, which he encountered in a dentist's office around the age of 11 or 12. A few years later, Edward FitzGerald's translation of *The Rubaiyat of Omar Khayyam* introduced Eliot to "a new world of feeling." He remembered the experience of reading that book as "a sudden conversion; the world appeared anew, painted with bright, delicious colours."[15] It was under the influence of *Omar* that Eliot wrote his earliest poetry–"a number of very gloomy and atheistical and despairing quatrains in the same style," long since lost.[16] Thereafter, he spent several years following "the usual adolescent course" through Romantic poetry: Lord Byron, Percy Bysshe Shelley, John Keats, Christina Rossetti, and Algernon Swinburne.[17] He later admitted to having an early appreciation for the supernatural in literature (citing Thomas De Quincey's *Confessions of an English Opium-Eater*, Robert Browning's "Childe Roland to the Dark Tower Came," and Gerard de Nerval's *Aurelia* as examples), as well as an early fondness for violent, sensationalistic Elizabethan and Jacobean drama.[18] His oldest extant poem, "A Lyric," was written a year or two later as an imitation of the 17th-century English poet Ben Jonson. Eliot remembered in 1959 that his English teacher was impressed and that his mother said, "it was a better poem than any she had written."[19] According to Eliot's friend Joseph Chiari, Charlotte Eliot "looked to him for the continuation and the fulfillment of both her passion for a moral and just life and her poetic gifts."[20] In 1910, she wrote to her son that she hoped he would succeed where she had failed. From that point on, T. S. had a mission.

Harvard and Poetry

Eliot entered Harvard University as an undergraduate in the fall of 1906. In years to come, he would rail against the liberalism of the Harvard elective system of the day, which allowed undergraduates to design their own curriculum. Taking cues from his classical studies professor Irving Babbitt, Eliot claimed that this type of liberalism contributed to aimlessness. During his freshman year, however, Eliot floundered. He enrolled in a wide array of classes in literature, history, and government, but failed to focus adequately on any of them. As a result, at the end of his first semester, he was placed on academic probation. This forced him to focus; he quickly resolved to complete his undergraduate course in three years, and then to pursue a master's degree in English literature.

During that time, Eliot continued to develop as a poet. He joined the staff of *The Advocate*, Harvard's undergraduate literary journal, which published several of his poems (later collected in the posthumous volume *Poems Written in Early Youth*). Although Eliot later remembered staff meetings as "a round robin to see who could say the most sarcastic thing about the other man's work,"[21] he made one connection there that would profoundly affect his future. In the spring of 1908, a young Southerner named Conrad Aiken joined *The Advocate*. Aiken and Eliot hit it off immediately, due in part to their shared love of language and enthusiasm for the pop culture of the day—especially comics (Krazy Kat, Mutt and Jeff, Nell Brinkley, and Rube Goldberg). Aiken later recalled that he and Eliot were both striving to find a "new poetic language [...] something less poetic, more inclusive, more quotidian, admitting even the vernacular, and lower in pitch: a new poetic voice, one in which one could *think*."[22]

According to Eliot, most aspiring poets at Harvard were focusing their attention on decadent English poets of the 1890s like Algernon Charles Swinburne, Oscar Wilde, Ernest Dowson, and John Davidson. Eliot himself drew some inspiration from Davidson's "Thirty Bob a Week," which showed him how to utilize the dingy urban images stored in his memory. Although Davidson's poem continued to haunt Eliot for years to come, it did not provide the impetus he needed to create something new. Eliot remembered, "The question was still: where do we go from Swinburne? And the answer appeared to be, nowhere."[23]

Eliot eventually found what he was looking for in December 1908, when he stumbled upon a book of French literary criticism. In the years to come, he acknowledged that the discovery of Arthur Symons' *The Symbolist Movement in Literature* (1899) was the single most important event in his development as a poet because it showed him that "there was a modern idiom, and that English poetry still had some unexplored possibilities."[24] Symons's book introduced Eliot to the poetry of Stéphane Mallarmé, Charles Baudelaire, Arthur Rimbaud, Paul Verlaine, Tristan Corbière and–most importantly–Jules Laforgue. Eliot's subsequent poems–"Conversation Galante," "Portrait of a Lady," the first two "Preludes," and a host of pieces posthumously published in *Inventions of the March Hare*–were, according to Eliot himself, "almost pure Laforgue, with a little Baudelaire."[25] These poems show Eliot experimenting with ironic detachment, and emulating a series of voices as he struggled to find his own.

Eliot was so invigorated by the influence of French poetry that he made arrangements to study in Paris during the 1910-1911 academic year. Conrad Aiken later remembered that "an editor of the *Advocate* had returned from Paris, after a year, in exotic Left Bank clothing, and with his hair parted behind: it had made a sensation."[26] Eliot, at least, seems to have taken notice. In his breakthrough poem "The Love Song of J. Alfred Prufrock," the poet wrote, "Shall I part my hair behind?" It was one of the many indecisions that haunted the titular character as he straddled a dark road between the old world and something new. Eliot was likewise poised between worlds–between America, the home of his youth, and Europe, where he would live out his adult life. Although he later suggested that his teacher Irving Babbitt influenced him to go to Paris, there is little doubt that Eliot went primarily as a poet in search of inspiration. In 1944 he wrote, "For many years France had represented above all, in my eyes, *poetry*."[27]

Paris and Philosophy

Ironically, when Eliot arrived in Paris in the fall of 1910, he found that French poetry was "somewhat in eclipse."[28] That did not, however, diminish the vivacity of the place for him. For Eliot, the ancient and cosmopolitan city itself was a work of art, the likes of which he had never previously experienced or imagined. Revolutionary new ideas in the fields of psychology, sociology, and philosophy colored the young poet's experiences there, and everything seemed to be woven together in a brilliant tapestry by the "spider-like figure" of philosopher Henri Bergson.[29]

Bergson's most famous book *Creative Evolution* had been published in 1907, and its success bolstered attendance for a series of lectures at the Collège de France in early 1911. Eliot was among those who witnessed the charismatic philosopher's live thought experiments, which one attendee described as follows: "For an hour, every Friday, at the Collège de France, a man was thinking, was creating in front of us. Through an effort of his entire being, he forced himself to recapture the original, the first, feeling and then to reconstitute it in a sort of vision in which he sought to express in multiple images, more and more precise, more and more subtle, what each one of us must find in the depths of ourselves, behind the screen of the superficial and conventional."[30]

Eliot declared that only those who had attended the lectures could comprehend the excitement of Bergsonism, and the poet himself was more than excited. He later claimed that he was temporarily converted to Bergson's philosophy, which attributed cosmic significance to poetic intuitions. Bergson's way of thinking influenced many of Eliot's poems from that period, especially "Rhapsody on a Windy Night" and "The Love Song of J. Alfred Prufrock." In the former, the poet mused:

The memory throws up high and dry
A crowd of twisted things;
A twisted branch upon the beach
Eaten smooth, and polished
As if the world gave up
The secret of its skeleton,
Stiff and white.
A broken spring in a factory yard,
Rust that clings to the form that the strength has left
Hard and curled and ready to snap.[31]

Both poems were completed in 1911 and can be read as Bergsonian stream-of-consciousness imagism fused with some of Eliot's other Parisian influences.

In addition to Laforgue and Baudelaire, there are also traces of Russian novelist Fyodor Dostoevsky. Eliot read *Crime and Punishment*, *The Idiot*, and *The Brothers Karamazov* during his winter in Paris, and the psychological complexities of these novels made a deep impression on him. An even more obvious influence was Charles-Louis Philippe's novel *Bubu of Montparnasse*, which Eliot read soon after his arrival in Paris, and which became for him a representative snapshot of Paris in 1910-1911. Philippe's novel, about a naïve student who falls in love with a syphilitic prostitute, defines Paris as "a weary dog [...] chasing a bitch in heat."[32] A comparatively primal sexuality imbues Prufrock's stream-of-consciousness journey. For the sake of comparison, here is Philippe, as translated by Laurence Vail:

On certain nights, having studied until eleven, he closed his books and sat crushed with sadness before all their knowledge. All the diplomas in the world were not worth the joy of life. Two or three visions of women he had encountered came to his mind, and he followed them, at first merely to divert himself. Then all the fire of his twenty years flared to life, and his senses felt the magic contained in a passing woman. He lept up, his throat parched, his heart contracted. He blew out the lamp and went out into the street.[33]

And here is Eliot, essentially continuing the narrative:

Let us go then, you and I,
When the evening is spread out against the sky
Like a patient etherized upon a table;
Let us go, through certain half-deserted streets,
The muttering retreats
Of restless nights in one-night cheap hotels
And sawdust restaurants with oyster-shells:

Streets that follow like a tedious argument
Of insidious intent
To lead you to an overwhelming question...

Oh, do not ask, "What is it?"
Let us go and make our visit.[34]

Although "Prufrock" would not be published until 1915, the composition of the poem in 1911 represented a creative turning point for Eliot. When Conrad Aiken read it, he began referring to his friend's poetry in terms of "the earlier Lamia kind"—a reference to the recurrent demonization of women in the Laforgian inventions—and "the later Prufrock variety."[35] Aiken saw not only new themes, but also a technical accomplishment; he claimed that Eliot had "adumbrated a form which might be exactly the solution [we] were all looking for—something freer, certainly, than the strictly stanzaic, or the monotonies of classic blank verse; with varying length of line, and, to some degree, a substitution of cadence for metrical beat or measure; but using both these and rhyme, too, when it wished, or when it suited."[36]

Eliot too realized that Paris had been good for his poetry, and he contemplated settling down there and trying to become a bilingual poet. In the end, however, the experience of encountering Bergson as a lecturer steered him back to Harvard, to pursue a Ph.D. in philosophy. He spent the next two years immersed in studies of Sanskrit and Pali literature—part of a deeply personal investigation into the underlying nature of metaphysical reality—and eventually "shunted Bergson down the hill" (according to Conrad Aiken) in favor of idealist philosopher F. H. Bradley.[37]

Eliot's student essays, recently published for the first time, illustrate an intense preoccupation with sacred texts of India (especially the *Upanishads* and the *Bhagavad Gita*) and the Buddhist Pali canon. There is no question that his Eastern studies exerted a strong influence on his future poetry, but despite his latent sympathy for the subject matter and a lifelong attachment to

Eastern symbolism (the lotus flower, Buddha's "fire sermon," etc.), he did not embrace the mysteries behind the texts. In 1933 he explained why, articulating his belief that "the only hope of really penetrating to the heart of the mystery would lie in forgetting how to think and feel as an American or a European: which, for practical as well as sentimental reasons, I did not wish to do."[38]

Instead, Eliot undertook a self-directed study of Christian saints and mystics, and the psychology of religious experiences within the Western tradition. He took extensive notes on books including William James' *The Varieties of Religious Experience*, Dean Inge's *Studies of English Mystics*, and Evelyn Underhill's *Mysticism*; his studies inspired a lifelong interest in the writings of Spanish mystic St. John of the Cross (especially *Dark Night of the Soul* and *The Ascent of Mount Carmel*) and English mystic Dame Julian of Norwich. Both of these Christian mystics became a lasting influence on Eliot's poetry and his spiritual life. For the time being, however, he was hesitant to devote himself to any particular religion, and remained more committed to philosophy in general.

In mid-1913, Eliot turned his attention to F. H. Bradley's 1893 book, *Appearance and Reality*. Although he would ultimately reject Bradley's ideas, Eliot thoroughly absorbed the philosopher's writing style during two intense years of study, one at Harvard and one at Oxford University in England. A decade later, he professed his admiration for the "magnificent austerity" of Bradley's prose, and the philosopher's "classic balance" of thought and feeling became the model for all of Eliot's critical writing.[39] Eliot similarly praised Harold Joachim, the Oxford mentor who guided him as he wrote his doctoral dissertation on Bradley, saying in 1938, "He taught me that one should know exactly what one meant before venturing to put words to paper, and that one should avoid metaphor whenever a plain statement can be found."[40]

While writing his dissertation, however, Eliot had begun to have doubts that anyone could ever know exactly what one meant. As he examined Bradley's conclusion that "Reality is spiritual" and cannot be fully comprehended by the scientific mind, Eliot realized that he was not willing to concede that philosophy leads inevitably to religion. In early 1915, he remained in limbo between two disciplines. At that time, the would-be philosopher wrote to a Harvard colleague that he had become something of a relativist, and was "ready to admit that the lesson of relativism is: to avoid philosophy and devote oneself to either *real* art or *real* science."[41] He then resolved to turn his dissertation into a criticism of Bradley's philosophy rather than a straightforward explication of it. Eliot's friend Stephen Spender suggested that at that point the poet became "occupied in exploiting Bradley for the purposes of writing his own poetry."[42] It would be more than a year before he delivered his completed dissertation to the philosophy department at Harvard. By then, his faith in institutional philosophy had eroded, leaving a void.

London and War

World War I was instrumental in Eliot's gradual transformation from philosophy student to professional poet. In August 1914, Germany declared war on Russia and Eliot found himself stranded in the German town of Marburg for two weeks, studying the work of phenomenologist Edmund Husserl. By September he was in London, where he wrote to his cousin Eleanor Hinkley about the shocking reality of a war that was threatening the lives of friends he'd made in Paris and Germany. His Parisian tutor Alain-Fournier was killed in battle that same month; he was 27, only two years older than Eliot.

In London, Conrad Aiken urged Eliot to call on Ezra Pound, a fellow poet and American ex-pat who was engaged in promoting new literary forms and movements, including *vers libre*, Imagism and Vorticism. Pound's prescription for modern poetry demanded precise language, meaningful rhythms, and classical precision. He found what he was looking for in the work of the French Symbolists, Dante, and Eliot's earliest experiments. After Eliot showed him "The

Love Song of J. Alfred Prufrock," Pound wrote to publisher Harriet Monroe that it was "the best poem I have yet had or seen from an American," and marveled that Eliot had "trained himself *and* modernized himself *on his own*."[43] He earnestly hoped that "Prufrock" was not a one-hit-wonder.

Eliot meanwhile wrote to Aiken, "I have done nothing good since ["Prufrock"] and writhe in impotence."[44] The new poems he composed during this period—"The Burnt Dancer," "The Love Song of St. Sebastian," "The Death of Saint Narcissus," and early fragments of *The Waste Land*—reveal his intense preoccupation with religious imagery and asceticism. From the poet's perspective, however, the poems lacked the right kind of intensity. Eliot was seeking a particular kind of stimulation to cure his "impotence."

The young poet briefly contemplated returning to Boston to pursue a career as a college professor, while pining for Emily Hale, a young American actress he had met in 1912 and declared his love to in the spring of 1914. Anticipating a dead end in America, he instead found himself walking the streets of London at night—like Prufrock and his predecessor in *Bubu of Montparnasse*—searching for a more immediate solution to his problem. Ever mindful of his grandfather's warnings about the social evil of prostitution, he suffered from a series of "nervous sexual attacks." Eliot explained to Aiken: "One walks about the streets with one's desires, and one's refinement rises up like a wall whenever opportunity approaches. I should be better off, I sometimes think, if I had disposed my virginity and shyness several years ago: and indeed I still think sometimes that it would be well to do so before marriage."[45]

Eliot's moral inculcation—his inherited sense "of what was done and not done"—created a situation in which the only outlet for his desires was his writing. The poet appeared at his bawdiest in private sketches of the period, including a series of "improper" verses about priapic King Bolo and his restless natives. These poems, circulated only among (male) friends, granted some freedom of expression to Eliot's most carnal urges—but not enough. Like the tragic hero of

Bubu, he yearned for real sexual experience. Like Prufrock, he could not act and felt destined to drown in a world of imagination.

Then, in the spring of 1915, a solution presented itself. In a letter to his cousin Eleanor Hinkley, Eliot wrote that he had met a few young women at a dancing party, and found them to be strikingly different from the women he'd met in America. He recorded the name of one lady in particular: Vivienne. A few weeks later, he was married to her.

2. The Waste Land

Vivienne

In the final years of his life, T. S. Eliot struggled to articulate the reasons for his marriage to Vivienne Haigh-Wood. "I was very immature for my age, very timid, very inexperienced," he wrote in a private paper in the 1960s, explaining that all he really wanted from her was "a flirtation or a mild affair."[1] According to a letter written to a colleague in 1915, the marriage had been "accelerated by events connected with the war."[2] What these "events" were is anyone's guess. They may have had something to do with straitened circumstances of the Haigh-Wood family or with the fact that Vivienne's younger brother Maurice was leaving to fight, or with the abrupt departure of Vivienne's previous suitor. Whatever the case, the couple's union seemed felicitous. The poet wanted to "burn my boats and commit myself to staying in England," and Vivienne thought she could "save the poet by keeping him in England."[3]

For a brief time, they might have been happy. Their mutual friend Brigit Patmore later remembered that Vivienne "shimmered with intelligence" in those early days, offering "a personality suited to [Eliot's] quiet elegance."[4] She also recalled a moment when she observed Eliot physically supporting his wife "with real tenderness," demonstrating his commitment to her "chosen work," which was dancing.[5] Vivienne herself later remembered how, in the early days of marriage, she and her husband would walk the streets of London at night together, planning their future. Unfortunately, the marital bliss was short-lived.

Within a few weeks, T. S. Eliot wrote to his brother that he felt revitalized, but that his wife was ill. By then, he had learned some very troubling details about the health of the woman he'd married. Eliot's friend Osbert Sitwell remembered, "She had never mentioned to him the appallingly bad health from which she had suffered even as a small child. She had been afflicted by tuberculosis of the bones, or a form of it, and had undergone so many operations before she was seven, that she was able to recall nothing until she reached that age."[6] Subsequently, Vivienne developed a nervous condition. When she was 16, a doctor recommended bromide—used in the 19th and early 20th centuries as an anticonvulsant and sedative—to help alleviate her symptoms. Over time, the drug probably exacerbated her condition. By the time she met Eliot, Vivienne was suffering from chronic "nerve storms" accompanied by frequent nausea, fevers, and migraines. Her health would only worsen in the years to come. Sitwell remembered: "Tom considered that since he possessed no means of his own at the time [...] she should have told him, and thus have prepared him in advance for her later illnesses, which were to impose so crushing an additional burden on him during many years."[7] The implication is that, to some degree, Eliot felt as if he had been tricked into marrying her. Other accounts of the marriage reinforce this perspective, depicting Vivienne as a manipulative seductress. When author Aldous Huxley met her in 1917, he observed that "it is almost entirely a sexual nexus between Eliot and her," and described Vivienne as "an incarnate provocation."[8] Eliot memoirist Robert Sencourt, who met the couple in 1926, suggested that "impressionable men" were helpless "under the spell of her fragile, mercurial vivacity."[9] Such accounts depict Vivienne as the victimizer, but she was also a victim.

Vivienne's biographer Carole Seymour-Jones has suggested that the pattern of illness during the early years of her marriage is closely linked to a relationship between the Eliots and Bertrand Russell. Russell had entered Eliot's life several years earlier when he was a visiting professor at Harvard. At that time, in his poem "Mr. Apollinax," Eliot characterized the renowned philosopher as a priapic interloper with devilish ears. Nevertheless, on July 9, 1915, Eliot invited Russell to dinner and introduced him to his new bride. Russell reported that Vivienne took to him immediately, and confided in him about the most intimate details of her new marriage: "She says she married him to stimulate him, but finds she can't do it."[10] Russell's subsequent declaration that the couple's "pseudo-honeymoon" was "a ghastly failure" has led to much speculation about the sexual relationship between the Eliots, but the statement could be little more than a veiled excuse for Russell's exploitation of their marital woes.[11]

Soon after, Eliot sailed to America to explain the hasty marriage to his parents–and to ask for their financial support. Vivienne, who was afraid to travel by sea, remained in London, where Russell resolved to "help" the couple through their troubles by lavishing affection and gifts on the insecure wife. Vivienne apparently was beguiled by the attention, as he knew she would be. She reported–to jealous former lover–"He is all over me, is Bertie, and I simply love him."[12] Writing to his former lover Ottoline Morrell at about the same time, Russell summed up the situation from his perspective: "I think she will fall more or less in love with me, but that can't be helped."[13]

When Eliot returned to England in mid-September 1915, he was rejoining (whether knowingly or not) what Vivienne characterized as a "triple ménage."[14] Russell employed Vivienne as his secretary, and shared a flat with her during the week while Eliot taught at the elite Highgate Junior School in north London. Russell maintained (in his ongoing letters to Ottoline Morrell) that he was performing "the purest philanthropy," loving Eliot like a son and Vivienne like a daughter.[15] The arrangement continued until the fall of 1917 when Russell confided in his new lover (the actress Colette O'Neil) that a recent tryst with Vivienne had been "*utter hell*."[16] After that, he began to withdraw from the Eliots' life.

In the years to come, the couple experimented with numerous therapies and medical solutions in an attempt to "cure" Vivienne's nervous condition. Nothing seemed to work, leaving both partners feeling frustrated and hopeless. At that point, the marriage became a torturous tragedy, with Vivienne playing the role of mad harpy and Eliot trying desperately to quell or ignore her. Osbert Sitwell remembered: "She had developed a capacity, derived equally from observation and a flair founded on instinct, for wounding and angering her husband, and in this showed a certain malign comprehension of his nature." As for Eliot's response, Sitwell said, "I had observed how solicitous he was for Vivienne, how patient with her, behaving to her, even during her most irresponsible moments in public, with a rather formal courtesy. Indeed, he seemed anxious to carry the whole weight of the marriage on his shoulders."[17] Because "poor Tom" appeared so decorous and responsible, while Vivienne appeared so cruel and manipulative, their friends generally pitied him and reviled her. Behind closed doors, her mental health continued to deteriorate. Eliot, meanwhile, focused his attention on his work.

It is not clear if or when he learned the details of his wife's affair with Russell, but many years later he wrote to Ottoline Morrell that Russell had "done Evil." He went on to cite the "spectacle of Bertie" as a "contributing influence" to his religious conversion in 1927.[18] In the years leading up to that turning point, the deeply troubled marriage produced "the state of mind out of which came *The Waste Land*."[19]

Ghost Sense

At the same time, he was taking advantage of his friend's troubled marriage, Russell was helping Eliot start a career as a critic and journalist. He introduced Eliot to the editors of the *International Journal of Ethics*, *The Monist*, and *The New Statesman*, who published the poet's earliest critical musings on philosophy, religion, and literature. By the fall of 1916, Eliot was struggling to balance his new teaching career with an ambitious commitment to journalism. He wrote to his mother that he needed to review six books a day to make ends meet financially. His friend Aldous Huxley observed that he was "terribly overworked fourteen hours a day."[20]

Eliot was also burdened by the constant pressures of living in wartime London. Ezra Pound's biographer John Tytell wrote that the atmosphere of the place had become visibly oppressive: "Streetlamps were blackened to dim the light or they were painted deep orange, creating a lurid, phantasmagoric effect. On air-raid nights, even the lighting of a match was forbidden."[21] On one occasion, when Eliot was working late into the night, he received a summons for showing too much light through his curtains during a government-imposed blackout. By then, the war had become inescapably personal for him. He had recently received word that Jean Verdenal, a French medical student he'd befriended during his year in Paris, had been killed in battle. Vivienne's brother Maurice also brought home the horrors of war, sharing gruesome details of sleepless nights among human remains in front-line trenches. These details enhanced the poet's sense of despair.

In the spring of 1917, Eliot was eager for some change, and Vivienne's family helped him to secure a desk job at Lloyd's Bank in London. Compared to the demands of teaching, he later said, the 9-to-5 bank job was "a rest cure."[22] It allowed him to invest more time and intellectual energy into his writing. Vivienne noticed the difference right away, and documented the completion of five new poems in the course of one week. Eliot shared the poems—some in English, some in French—with Huxley, who reported that "he is experimenting in a new genre" of "philosophical obscenity."[23] Eliot later explained that writing in French had freed him from writer's block.

One of Eliot's coworkers recalled that, during his time at Lloyd's Bank, the poet "seemed to be living in a dreamland... he would often in the middle of dictating a letter break off suddenly, grasp a sheet of paper and start writing quickly when an idea came to him."[24] Fellow literary critic I. A. Richards claimed that Eliot was "almost a haunted being" during this time, "living seemingly many lives."[25] Eliot himself mused that he sometimes sensed that his life was unreal, like "one of Dostoevsky's novels [...] it all seems like a dream."[26] And like Dostoevsky, Eliot claimed to believe that man belongs to two worlds: one physical and one spiritual. In the "real" world, a man would watch troops departing for war from Waterloo Station and wonder if it was some kind of hallucination. In the other world, those troops were shades in Dante's Inferno. In the strange half-world of wartime London, Eliot could likewise find himself simultaneously bored with the mundane world around him and terrified on the doorstep of the invisible Absolute. Later, he would recall attending a dinner party on a night when an air-raid seemed imminent, and the atmosphere was one of ominous silence and stillness. The experience inspired his poem "Sweeney among the Nightingales," which he regarded as his most serious work in years.

The poem introduced a character who reappears in many of Eliot's works between 1918 and 1927—first in the short poems "Sweeney Erect" and "Mr. Eliot's Sunday Morning Service," and later in *The Waste Land* and the aborted "jazz play" *Sweeney Agonistes*. Conrad Aiken proposed that the Sweeney character was based on an ex-pugilist who gave Eliot boxing lessons in Boston, and Eliot himself later described Sweeney as a pugilist-turned-bartender. By the time he gave the latter description, the poet had completed his cycle of Sweeney stories, and the character had evolved from a simple (at least, simple-minded) figure in a still-life into a madman haunted by the metaphysical reality of sin and damnation. Sweeney's evolution parallels and in some ways illuminates Eliot's poetic and spiritual development during the years leading up to his religious conversion.

In a 1918 essay, the poet wrote that one of the great achievements of the recently-deceased American novelist Henry James (1843–1916) was having given "substance" to Nathaniel Hawthorne's "ghost-sense."[27] Whereas Hawthorne's narrative voice affirmed the existence of supernatural forces in colonial New England, James instead depicted the psychological legacy of early American puritanism through the thoughts and actions of his characters. Later, Eliot suggested that Hawthorne's work was "best appreciated by the reader with Calvinism in his bones and witch-hanging (not witch-hunting) on his conscience."[28] He was no doubt thinking of Henry James, whose novels (particularly *The Sense of the Past*) made

Hawthorne's "ghost sense" real for Victorian readers, as well as himself. According to Virginia Woolf, Eliot initially aspired to develop artistically "in the manner of Henry James," perhaps by making Hawthorne's ghost-sense real for the modernist era.[29] Over time, Eliot became increasingly conscious of both writers' preoccupations with spiritual reality. When he eventually abandoned that avenue of development, he concluded: "The essential thing [is] their indifference to religious dogma at the same time as their exceptional awareness of spiritual reality."[30]

By then, Eliot had come to an identical conclusion about the character of Sweeney, and about his own early poetry. According to Virginia Woolf, he decided that he needed to pursue a different path of development, by describing "externals" instead of Hawthorne and Joyce's "internals."[31] He would make his ghosts flesh and blood.

The Sacred Wood

At the same time, Eliot was developing a heightened awareness of spiritual reality, he was also forming a critical theory that would help him to express and examine it consciously. In his development as a critic, perhaps no writer exerted a greater influence on him than John Middleton Murry. Eliot met Murry in March 1919, when Murry asked him to be his assistant editor on a London periodical called *The Athenaeum*. Eliot turned down the job, but a friendship grew around common interests. Eliot became a regular and enthusiastic contributor to the journal and, within a few months, he was writing to Murry that knowing him had become a "great event."[32] By that time, Eliot may have realized that in Murry he had found a kind of critical foil, whose writings could help Eliot to clarify and distinguish his own contrary beliefs and ideological positions.

Moved by the classicism of Irving Babbitt, Ezra Pound, and fellow poet T. E. Hulme, Eliot was at that time pushing for a modern-day revival of "classical ideals." In 1917, he defined this revival in terms of "*form* and *restraint* in art, *discipline* and *authority* in religion, *centralization* in government (either as socialism or monarchy)."[33] Around that same time, while teaching survey courses at Highgate and then the Royal Grammar School in High Wycombe, and later, while delivering nighttime extension lectures at the University of London, he outlined a whirlwind review of the whole of English literature for himself and his students. In the end, he came to some definite conclusions about historical periods of strength and weakness regarding classical ideals.

In the fall of 1919, when he began to make a formal written assessment of the entire English literary tradition in a series of critical essays, he also started to establish a creed for his future work as both a critic and a poet. In stark opposition to John Middleton Murry, Eliot declared himself an anti-romantic. To Eliot, the Romantic era of English literature (which he said had peaked in the first half of the 19th century) was a period of emotional excess and intellectual chaos, and he wanted to make a critical assault on the popularity of the Romantic writers. With that in mind, he started developing an idiosyncratic notion of "classical" poetry, which he illustrated in a series of essays for an American literary journal called *The Egoist*. These essays later became the basis for his first book of literary criticism, *The Sacred Wood*, which would, in turn, become a manifesto for 20th century Neoclassicism.

The ideas in Eliot's most famous early essay, "Tradition and the Individual Talent," had been germinating in the poet's mind over the course of several years of emotional chaos in his marital life. In 1917, he had written in a private letter that he liked to think of a writer as "perfectly cool and detached, regarding other people's feelings or his own, like a God who has got beyond them."[34] In 1919, he observed that "the progress of an artist is continual self-sacrifice, a continual extinction of personality."[35] "Tradition and the Individual Talent" espoused an impersonal theory of poetry, based on Eliot's newfound belief that poetry should be an escape from personal emotion rather than a romantic indulgence of emotion. Later in life, the poet admitted to fellow author E. M. Forster that this theory probably stemmed from "personal motives."[36] At the time, however, Eliot's psychic survival–to say nothing of his literary legacy–was built on his ability to turn personal chaos into universal art.

In the subsequent essay "Hamlet and His Problems," Eliot provided his formula for such transformations. He wrote that "the only way of expressing emotion in the form of art is by finding an 'objective correlative,'" which he defined as "a set of objects, a situation, a chain of events which shall be the formula of that *particular* emotion."[37] Using Shakespeare's *Hamlet* as a negative illustration of his theory, the young poet boldly declared that Shakespeare had failed to find an objective correlative for the "stuff" he wanted to "drag to light."[38] Eliot later admitted that he had intended to be deliberately provocative by criticizing Shakespeare's most famous play, but he also explained that in his youth he was more heavily influenced by the Bard's peers, especially John Webster, Cyril Tourneur, and Thomas Middleton. Those were the dramatists who showed Eliot how to drag his own "stuff" to light.

In *The Sacred Wood*, Eliot praised these particular Jacobean dramatists as representatives of a lost poetic tradition that emphasized "a quality of sensuous thought, or of thinking through the senses, or of the senses thinking."[39] He expanded his celebration of this tradition in his 1921 essay "The Metaphysical Poets," which criticizes certain Romantic poets (namely, Alfred Lord Tennyson and Robert Browning) for failing to "feel their thought as immediately as the odour of a rose," while praising the Jacobean dramatists and their 17th-century successors (particularly John Donne) for finding "the verbal equivalent for states of mind and feeling." Eliot elaborated on the ideal circumstances for writing metaphysical poetry: "When a poet's mind is perfectly equipped for its work, it is constantly amalgamating disparate experience; the ordinary man's experience is chaotic, irregular, fragmentary. The latter falls in love, or reads Spinoza, and these two experiences have nothing to do with each other, or with the noise of a typewriter or the smell of cooking; in the mind of the poet these experiences are always forming new wholes."[40] Eliot claimed that in the later part of the 17th century (beginning with the work of John Milton) a "dissociation of sensibility" set in, from which English literature had not recovered.

Eliot obviously saw himself as a living member of the lost metaphysical tradition, and he hoped to help revive it in the 20th century–through both his critical writing and his poetry. When editor Bruce Richmond commissioned him to write a series of essays on Elizabethan and Jacobean poets for the London *Times Literary Supplement*, Eliot seized the opportunity to continue his study of metaphysical poetry. Around the same time, in the 1920 essay "Modern Tendencies in Poetry," he laid out his own poetic goal: to create a worthy amalgamation of past and present, thought and feeling, tradition and the individual talent.

Myths and Mystery

Between March 1918 and December 1920, James Joyce's modernist novel *Ulysses* appeared in serialized form in *The Egoist*, the American journal that had also published Eliot and briefly employed him as an editor. Virginia Woolf wrote exasperatedly in her diary that Eliot rated *Ulysses* "on par with *War & Peace*!"[41] Although the poet later clarified that he did not believe that *Ulysses* "gave a new insight into human nature," he argued that it was "a step toward making the modern world possible for art."[42] What Joyce's novel gave to the modern world, according to Eliot, was a technique for amalgamating experience. Eliot called it the mythical method, and he saw it as a way to combine the order of mythmaking with the perceived chaos of modern life, without needing to explain the relationship. Woolf recorded in her diary that Eliot said, "Explanation is unnecessary. If you put it in, you dilute the facts. You should feel these without explanation."[43]

In *Ulysses*, Joyce fused Homer's *Odyssey* with contemporary life in Dublin, through the combination of experimental narrative techniques and literary allusion. Eliot did something similar in his poems "Sweeney among the Nightingales" (1918) and "Sweeney Erect" (1919), which juxtaposed images and phrases from classical Greek mythology with images and phrases from contemporary life. "Gerontion," a short but important poem that Eliot began writing in 1917 and completed in early 1919, went further—arising out of a blend of personal feelings, experience, and new reading, and hinting at transcendent unity. Eliot wanted to achieve the same effect on a much grander scale, and perhaps even provide new insight into human nature.

In the fall of 1919, Eliot began corresponding with friends and family members about a long poem he had in mind. For nearly two years he struggled with visions and revisions, but he did not have the time or the focus to complete such a serious and lengthy work. His wife's health continued to deteriorate, exacting a significant physical and psychological toll on both of them. In March 1921, he wrote to a friend that Vivienne had become delusional. A few months later, she herself candidly told one of her friends that she felt as if she was going mad.

That summer, Eliot's mother and brother came to visit the couple in London. During their visit, Vivienne displayed the erratic behavior of a paranoiac—constantly moving among three rented flats in London, in order to avoid detection. Henry observed that his brother was also beginning to seem mentally unstable, and in desperate need of rest and solitude for the sake of his own sanity. When his relatives returned to America, Eliot became despondent. He wrote to Henry, "Your having been here seems very real, and your not being here but in Chicago seems as unreal as death."[44] Eliot seems to have been having his own difficulties distinguishing between reality and delusion. By then, he had already gone to see a neurologist, who recommended a three-month rest cure for what he and Vivienne both characterized as a nervous breakdown.

On October 14, the Eliots traveled to the seaside town of Margate for a prescribed month of rest and recuperation. At the end of the month, Vivienne returned to London alone. During this period of respite, away from the pressures of his marriage and his work,

Eliot was finally able to focus on his long poem. In the first week of November he completed a first draft of "The Fire Sermon," the third section of *The Waste Land*, concluding on a note of ritualistic purification:

'On Margate Sands.
I can connect
Nothing with nothing.
The broken fingernails of dirty hands.
My people humble people who expect
Nothing.'
la la

To Carthage then I came

Burning burning burning burning
O Lord Thou pluckest me out
O Lord Thou pluckest

burning[45]

At that time, the poet realized that his recent breakdown was not a matter of nerves, but of an "aboulie," the French word for lack of will.[46] With "The Fire Sermon," he diagnosed his affliction in more distinctly religious terms, and accordingly, he began to seek a cure that had some religious context. Following the advice of friends, Eliot traveled to Switzerland to consult Dr. Roger Vittoz, a Catholic psychologist who employed essentially Indian and Buddhist meditation practices to rehabilitate nervous patients living in a dreamlike state.

By mid-December, Eliot wrote to his brother that he was learning how to calm his mind and focus his thoughts, which was a boon for his writing. In the final days of the year, he completed his first full draft of *The Waste Land*. According to Virginia Woolf, Eliot later told her that he wrote the last verses "in a trance—unconsciously."[47] This experience seems to have given the poet the confidence to speak authoritatively about so-called automatic writing, although he never recommended it as a method for literary composition, insisting that "no masterpiece can be produced whole by such means." In Eliot's experience, a "temporary crystallization of the mind" could take place at the end of a long journey, after the material of the poetry had been "incubating" within the poet for many months or years.[48] He maintained, however, that such a crystallization was not a mystical vision—not something delivered to the poet's mind from *outside*—but "a motion terminating in an arrangement of words on paper."[49] For the poet, *The Waste Land* was a personal terminus. Once it was delivered to the literary world, of course, it became something else.

In early January 1922, Eliot shared the first full draft of *The Waste Land* with Ezra Pound. The fellow artist recommended significant revisions to the poem (which are thoroughly documented in *The Waste Land: A Facsimile and Transcript*), but he nevertheless recognized the importance of the work and promptly declared *The Waste Land* "the justification of the 'movement,' of our modern experiment, since 1900."[50] Others were not as certain. Woolf, who heard the poem read aloud at a Bloomsbury dinner party in June 1922, reacted strongly to the *sound* of *The Waste Land*, but could not discern the *sense*. She reflected, "It has great beauty & force of phrase: symmetry, & tensity. What connects it together, I'm not so sure."[51]

The Waste Land was published simultaneously in England and America in the fall of 1922. Readers varied in their enthusiasm, but nearly everyone had a theory about what the poem meant. Some said it was about the war and the disillusionment of the post-war generation, while others identified it as a melancholy autobiography. Publisher Harold Monro offered the most astute contemporary summary: "*The Waste Land* is one metaphor with a multiplicity of interpretations."[52] Interpretation, he suggested, should be left to individual readers. Seemingly in agreement, Eliot initially avoided offering his own interpretation(s), beyond a few cryptic notes about the influence of mythologist Jessie Weston's book *From Ritual to Romance: Folklore, Magic and the Holy Grail* and cultural anthropologist James George Frazer's book *The Golden Bough: A Study in Magic and Religion*. Later, in 1931, Eliot all but dismissed *The Waste Land* as "a grouch against life."[53] In 1959, he explained: "One wants to get something off one's chest. One doesn't know quite what it is that one wants to get off the chest until one's got it off."[54] After that, he implied, it doesn't matter to the poet what he has gotten off his chest; he has already moved on to a new phase of exploration.

Literary critics refused to let the poet off the hook that easy—and, Eliot conceded, it was partly his own fault. In 1920, he had written that "immature poets imitate; mature poets steal."[55] He then provided an official record of his own thefts by including source notes in the U.S. edition of *The Waste Land*. His intention, as he later explained to I. A. Richards, was to prove the theory that "it is possible to increase the effect for the reader by letting him know a reference or a meaning."[56] He hoped readers would seek out the source of the allusion(s) and then return to the original work with greater knowledge, producing an enhanced experience of the original work. Instead, the notes seemed to encourage source-hunting over and above pure poetic effect. In 1956, the poet reflected, "I regret having sent so many enquirers off on a wild goose chase after Tarot cards and the Holy Grail."[57] He suggested that the poem might have been more effective—or, rather, affective—if he had allowed the mythical allusions therein to remain mysterious. He offered a particularly vivid analogy that compared the initial experience of an obscure poem to being surrounded by people who have no skin. "At first," he wrote, "it would be hard to get used to seeing people like that... It would be so entirely new." After a while, however, one would adapt to the sight and reconsider. Then, "you would find them, possibly, more interesting. Their eyes would be more expressive. The play of their muscles would be fascinating."[58] The poet regretted that he had robbed his readers of such an experience.

Today, many first-time readers approach *The Waste Land* as an expression of the zeitgeist surrounding World War I, but Eliot was always more inclined to view it within the context of his own poetic and spiritual development. In November 1922, he told colleagues that *The Waste Land* was as far behind him as "Prufrock," and that he was "now feeling toward a new form and style."[59] Two months later he described the epic poem as a "consummation" of his past work, and girded himself for the future: "It will take me all my courage and persistence, and perhaps a long time, to do something better. But 'something' must be better."[60] His brother Henry offered this warning: "I expect your next poem to be either finer or much more obscure and perverse. Heaven direct your steps."[61] His mother Charlotte was even more prophetic. She wrote that she would like to see her son "supplement *The Waste Land* by its natural sequence 'The coming of the Grail.'"[62]

3. Ash-Wednesday

Death's Dream Kingdom

In England, *The Waste Land* made its first appearance in the inaugural issue of *The Criterion*, a quarterly literary journal that strategically positioned Eliot's poem between the work of Fyodor Dostoevsky and James Joyce. Taken as a whole, the contents of the issue offered a compelling portrait of the modern Western mind–precisely what its editor intended. As editor-in-chief of *The Criterion*, Eliot aimed to bring together "the best in new thinking and new writing in its time, from all the countries of Europe that had anything to contribute to the common good."[1] The poet wanted to create something more than a literary magazine. In 1923, he had declared that the ideal function of a literary review was to "maintain the autonomy and disinterestedness of literature, and at the same time to exhibit the relations of literature–not to 'life,' as something contrasted to literature, but to all the other activities, which, together with literature, are the components of life."[2] In the years to come he would expand the scope of *The Criterion*–and his own critical writing–to include contemporary politics, economics, social theory, and above all religion.

Eliot's poetry would undergo a similar transformation during the following two decades. At first, as his brother had predicted, his poetry became more obscure and perverse, and for most of 1924, Eliot had trouble writing anything at all. Distracted and exhausted by the perpetual illness of his wife, he produced only a few meager essays between January and July. In August, he complained in a private letter that writer's block was squeezing him out like the walls of the torture chamber in Edgar Allan Poe's short story "The Pit and the Pendulum." Then, in September, he suddenly produced his first poems since *The Waste Land*: a trio of experiments that he called

"Doris's Dream Songs." Doris had appeared as a minor character at the end of his 1919 poem "Sweeney Erect." Strangely, she doesn't appear at all in her so-called "dream songs." For Eliot, the title signified an oblique but important connection in his own mind. He explained to Harold Monro, who published the three dream songs in November that they were not written for standalone publication, but for a different purpose which he declined to specify.

In a 1959 interview, Eliot referred to the first two dream songs ("Eyes that last I saw in tears" and "The wind sprang up at four o'clock") as "preliminary sketches."[3] Presumably, he regarded them as forerunners of either his 1925 poem *The Hollow Men*, which incorporated the third dream song, or *Sweeney Agonistes*, an experimental play featuring the Doris character, which he began writing over the course of two sleepless nights "with the aid of youthful enthusiasm and a bottle of gin."[4] The poet had begun contemplating the play in 1923, envisioning it as a modern-day drama featuring "an orchestra consisting exclusively of drums."[5] He had a notion that he could create a new form of poetic drama by using primitive rhythm to ritualistic effect–employing what he later termed "auditory imagination." In 1933, Eliot defined auditory imagination as "the feeling for syllable and rhythm, penetrating far below the conscious levels of thought and feeling, invigorating every word; sinking to the most primitive and forgotten, returning to the origin and bringing something back, seeking the beginning and the end."[6] When he started writing *Sweeney Agonistes*, Eliot was chasing a sound, something he heard in his dream-world that subliminally conveyed a sense of a mysterious and possibly transformative experience. To his mind's ear, it was the ominous sound of a monotonous drumbeat; to his critical mind, the sound was an intimation of the existence of another world: a hidden metaphysical reality that other poets had explored before him.

Eliot continued to assert his place in a long tradition of metaphysical poets. In a November 1924 lecture, he charted a path of recovery, from the modern derangement of Dostoevsky to the medieval unity of Dante. In Dostoevsky's novels, as in the work of

Nathaniel Hawthorne and Henry James, Eliot saw "two planes of reality, and that the scene before our eyes is only the screen and veil of another action which is taking place behind it." He wrote that Dostoevsky's characters are "partially aware" of the deeper reality and often in communication with voices of "spectres" from that other "Kingdom."[7] In *Sweeney Agonistes*, Eliot began a comparable poetic journey into "death's dream kingdom." Haunted by a prophecy of imminent death, his character Doris anticipates crossing over into the afterlife. Sweeney, meanwhile, contemplates–and, in an unpublished outline of the play, commits–an act of murder that makes him acutely aware of the other world. From that point forward, he exists in the dual reality of Dostoevsky's *Crime and Punishment*.

Years earlier, Eliot had contemplated the transformative effect of committing an act of murder, in a rare piece of prose fiction called "Eeldrop and Appleplex." In it, he wrote, "The important fact is that for the man the act [of murder] is eternal, and that for the brief space he has to live, he is already dead. He is already in a different world from ours. He has crossed the frontier."[8] The speaker in *The Hollow Men* has also crossed the frontier; he now exists completely in the otherworld of Dante's *Divine Comedy*.

In retrospect, it seems clear that a kind of preliminary religious conversion is taking place in these verses–one that can no more be reversed than death can be reversed. Eliot later claimed that his marriage to Vivienne became, during this period, "like a Dostoevsky novel written by [John] Middleton Murry."[9] To him, this description probably signified a particular kind of failure. Eliot regarded Murry as a self-indulgent Romantic, and Dostoevsky as an unsuccessful Classicist who had spent his life vainly resisting the impulse toward Romanticism–a movement that, according to Eliot, "accepted the divorce of human and divine, denied the divine, and asserted the perfection of the human to be divine."[10] By 1924, Eliot's preferred model was Dante, whose art represented for him "the most comprehensive, and the most *ordered* presentation of emotions that has ever been made."[11] Emphasizing the need to study the whole of

The Divine Comedy (not just the *Inferno*), he asserted that Dante's classical philosophy was superior to Dostoevsky's veiled romanticism. According to Eliot, Dante recognized that "neither human nor divine will be denied, that they are inseparable and eternally in conflict."[12] The recognition of this duality, he concluded, is the Catholic doctrine of Original Sin.

At this stage, Eliot was hesitant to assert either the truth or untruth of Dante's philosophy definitively, but his use of Dante's symbolism in *The Hollow Men* implies at least a strong interest in Catholic doctrine–just as his discarding of the preliminary "dream songs" (never reprinted as such) and *Sweeney Agonistes* (never completed) suggests a change of perspective. In 1936, Eliot wrote to his brother that *The Hollow Men* was his only blasphemous poem and that it represented "the lowest point I ever reached in my sordid domestic affairs."[13] Readers can only speculate about what made 1925 his "lowest point." Did Eliot perhaps dream of murdering his mentally-ill wife? Is that why he subsequently cultivated an abiding interest in murder mysteries, and in the criminal case of the notorious Dr. Crippen? (Friends reported that on two separate occasions Eliot attended costume parties dressed as the American-born dentist who brutally murdered his wife in their North London home.) Such speculations give rise to the possibility that Eliot's initial title for *Sweeney Agonistes*–"The Marriage of Life and Death"–might have been a sardonic play on words.

Whatever the case, Eliot certainly spent many years contemplating the repercussions–especially the moral-metaphysical ones–of committing murder. These contemplations prompted him to articulate his belief in the reality of sin and damnation. It may have been in light of this belief that he declared *The Hollow Men* a blasphemous poem. In *The Use of Poetry and the Use of Criticism*, Eliot wrote that genuine blasphemy is "the product of partial belief, and is as impossible to the complete atheist as to the perfect Christian. It is a way of affirming belief."[14] At least, for him it was. By 1925, Eliot was partly a Christian.

Anglo-Catholic in Religion

In 1928, at the age of 40, Eliot made a bold public declaration of his personal beliefs. "The general point of view," he wrote, "may be described as classicist in literature, royalist in politics, and anglo-catholic in religion."[15] Although he anticipated that his declaration might cause some confusion, he felt it necessary to articulate his "lines of development" in order to clarify his public image. He was *not* a modernist, nor was he the sly nihilist that some critics–and even friends–took him for. Moreover, he never had been.

As anticipated, many of his liberal-minded peers reacted strongly. Conrad Aiken publicly accused Eliot of "a complete abdication of intelligence,"[16] while Virginia Woolf privately lamented the thought that "poor dear Tom Eliot" was "dead to us all from this day forward."[17] Woolf shouldn't have been so surprised; she had recognized Eliot's religious inclinations many years earlier. In the spring of 1923, she wrote in her diary: "That strange figure Eliot dined here last night. I feel that he has taken the veil, or whatever monks do."[18] The poet's surrender simply took longer than she thought.

Eliot's religious conversion was also clearly foreshadowed in his writing. In a letter he wrote in 1917 to Bertrand Russell, he mentioned that he was "convinced that there is something beneath Authority in its historical forms which needs to be asserted clearly without reasserting impossible forms of political and religious organisation."[19] For years, he struggled to assert abstract ideals, but he kept returning to established political and religious ideologies. In 1923, he expressed enthusiasm about "the chance of establishing an austere classicism"[20] among those who were willing to pledge "allegiance to something outside themselves."[21] Without committing himself to any specific "outside Authority," Eliot went on to suggest that if "a man's interest is political, he must, I presume, profess an allegiance to principles, or to a form of government, or to a monarch; and if he is interested in religion, and has one, to a Church."[22]

By early 1925, Eliot's critical writing was following these lines. Around the time of *The Hollow Men*, John Middleton Murry nominated Eliot to give the prestigious annual Clark Lectures at Cambridge University. The poet called the invitation "a ray of hope just at *the blackest moment in my life*."[23] He intended to use the lectures as an opportunity to schematize an intellectual order, consciously constructed out of his own emotional chaos, and he hoped that the process of preparing and presenting them would keep his mind "together."[24] He chose as his topic Dante's metaphysical poetry, especially the *Vita Nuova*, which provided him with a template for his reflections on the possibility of a "new life" through a new type of love.

During the months of preparation, Eliot candidly told Murry about his desire to extract himself from his marriage to Vivienne. Living with such a volatile companion, the poet said, had forced him to turn himself into a kind of automaton–senses dulled, emotions suppressed for the sake of self-preservation. Eliot knew he could not continue to live like that without causing further (perhaps irreparable) damage to both himself and his wife. At the same time, he was reluctant to abandon Vivienne in an attempt to revive himself; he saw no way forward. Murry advised him that "nothing but harm can come of your trying to kill yourself to keep her alive."[25]

Eliot did not initiate a legal separation from his wife until 1933, but he began reorganizing his life much sooner. Haunted by an intense awareness of sin and damnation, he looked to the Church for moral support and guidance. In his Cambridge lectures, posthumously published as *The Varieties of Metaphysical Poetry*, Eliot recommended–for himself, as well as his readers–a disciplined return to the Catholic "unity" expressed in Dante's poetry. In his mind, it was the only viable solution to his personal crisis–but it was not an easy one.

Among those who celebrated Eliot's turn to Christianity were some who reported that it was merely a comforting re-turn to the

Christianity of his youth. Eliot vehemently denied this. In a 1926 letter to his brother, he complained that the liberal theology of his parents' and grandparents' Unitarianism had been "bad preparation for brass tacks like birth, copulation, death, hell, heaven and insanity," and a poor consolation for "a life like a bad Russian novel."[26] What Unitarianism lacked was dogma; it failed to acknowledge the metaphysical realities of sin and damnation. To him, the absence of dogma made Unitarianism tantamount to atheism—and he could take no comfort in atheism, regardless of any sentimental attachments he might have had to the religion of his youth.

Eliot did not want an easy, comforting religion; he needed help confronting the dark reality of his own experience. In 1932, he explained to his friend Stephen Spender, "I believe that the world will always be an unpleasant place, a place of trial for individual souls, and that the vast majority of its population will always be a compound of knave and blockhead, chiefly moved by vanity and fear, and kept quiet by laziness."[27] The chaos of this pessimistic view of humanity underpinned Eliot's felt need for an outside Authority, and for dogma, to fill what he described in 1929 as "the void that I find in the middle of all human happiness and all human relations."[28] Without the Church, he concluded, there could be no hope for redemption and no reconciliation to life. His perspective echoes the sentiments of the 17th-century Catholic theologian Blaise Pascal, who wrote that "the Christian faith goes mainly to establish these two facts, the corruption of nature, and redemption by Jesus Christ."[29] Perhaps that is why the poet regarded Pascal as the most relevant Christian writer of the modern age.

By 1926, Eliot saw a pattern of redemption emerging from his personal waste land. The development of his poetry appeared to be closely related to the teachings of the Catholic Church, and there are reasons to believe that Eliot almost became a Catholic around this time. In the spring, Eliot and his wife traveled to Rome with the poet's brother Henry and his new bride Theresa. There, the poet surprised everyone by falling to his knees at the entrance of St.

Peter's Basilica in the Vatican. None of his companions knew what to make of his behavior at the time.

Despite his apparent reverence for Catholicism, however, Eliot did not become a Roman Catholic. In the spring of 1927, he was studying doctrinal differences between Catholicism and Anglicanism, as well as the schism between Rome and Canterbury. Two decades earlier, the Pope had formally condemned the subversive influence of theological "Modernism," declaring that new, post-Darwin interpretations of Catholic doctrine were blasphemous, and at the same time rejecting the Anglican view of church-state relations. In the years that followed, Anglican intellectuals strove to reconcile faith and science for members of their communion, producing influential books like *Essays Catholic and Critical*—an anthology that Eliot was reading carefully in March 1927.[30] In personal correspondence with Eliot, Anglican clergyman (and fellow American expat) William Force Stead praised the book, opining that it reconciled the best of modern thought with High Anglican doctrine. Soon after, Eliot decided to become an Anglo-Catholic Anglican, a member of the English Church who strongly valued the religious-social tension between Catholic and Protestant elements within it.

One of the primary influences on his decision seems to have been his enthusiasm for the writings of 17th-century Anglican bishop Lancelot Andrewes—a learned, "high church" traditionalist who oversaw the translation of the King James Bible. Eliot was aware of Andrewes at least as early as 1919 when he mentioned the bishop in two separate book reviews, and William Force Stead reportedly stoked this interest during the early 1920s. He again referred to Andrewes in essays for *The Chapbook* (in 1921) and *The Criterion* (in 1924). By 1926, when the editor of the London *Times* asked him for an article on Andrewes, Eliot had come to regard him as something of an intellectual gatekeeper to the Church of England. He anticipated that writing the article would be "a pretty serious matter" for him, forcing him to "clear up my mind and try to come to conclusions [...] affecting my whole position."[31] In the article, which was published anonymously in September of that year, Eliot celebrated the spirit of Anglicanism in the Elizabethan era, and recommended Andrewes as a complement to Dante. According to his friend Robert Sencourt, however, the poet continued to "await more illumination."[32]

That same month, Eliot went with his wife to Divonne-les-Bains, a retreat in eastern France. There he met Sencourt, who later recalled, "Tom told me that he had never been a practicing Anglican and that there were one or two points he would have to settle before he could become one."[33] Sencourt referred Eliot to Charles Lindley Wood, the second Earl of Halifax, to help him settle his remaining conflicts. Lord Halifax was a prominent church leader dedicated to reviving Catholic principles within the Church of England, and to creating a formal dialogue between the Anglican Church and Rome. His views probably reinforced Eliot's perspective of the Anglican Church as "the Catholic Church in England," instead of as an English Church in which national politics would supersede religious dogma. According to Sencourt, Lord Halifax concluded that Eliot not only "believed everything a Catholic should believe," but also that his conversion to Anglicanism might–because of the poet's rhetorical gifts and cultural influences–"help to redeem the Church of England from its separation from Rome, and lead it back to Catholic unity."[34]

When Eliot returned to London in early January 1927, William Force Stead was equally hopeful that if the poet converted, "the old sickness from which literature has suffered since the days of Swinburne would take an immense leap forward toward health and strength again."[35] Eliot was not as optimistic as Lord Halifax about the future of Catholic unity, but he had long shared Stead's hopes for a classical literary revival–and he was willing to do whatever he could to make it happen. A few weeks later, Eliot asked for Stead's help in being confirmed, privately, as a member of the Anglican Church. At that time, in a minor essay on "literature, science and dogma" published in *The Dial*, he casually adopted (by paraphrasing) the Anglican doctrine that "man's chief end is to glorify God, and to enjoy him forever." In the same essay, he responded to a critic who suggested that poetry could be a means of salvation, arguing that such a declaration was like saying that "the wall-paper will save us when the walls have crumbled."[36] Although he would always remain thoroughly devoted to poetry, his perspective on the function of art had changed permanently.

The Time of Tension

On June 29, 1927, Rev. William Force Stead baptized Eliot in a private ceremony at Holy Trinity Church, an Anglican church in rural Finstock, Oxfordshire. Five months later Eliot applied for British citizenship. To some, it seemed as if he had undergone a sudden transformation, but for Eliot, these formal commitments represented only an intermediate stage of a journey that he had begun years earlier, and would continue for the rest of his life. The years 1927 to 1930—during which he wrote the first four Ariel poems (*Journey of the Magi*, *A Song for Simeon*, *Animula*, *Marina*) and *Ash-Wednesday*—represented for the poet a "time of tension" between his past and his future as a poet, a critic, and (most importantly) a Christian.

In a 1953 interview, Eliot said that he had thought he was finished as a poet after *The Hollow Men*. That poem had served as a capstone piece in the 1925 edition of his "complete works," which was published by Faber & Gwyer. In the same year, Eliot went to work as an editor for the small publishing house, and he would remain there for the rest of his professional life. When the firm inaugurated a series called "The Ariel Poems," Eliot promised to contribute something original to help bolster the series. This commitment, he explained in a 1953 interview, had "released the stream" that carried him toward his greatest works.[37]

Journey of the Magi, the first poem Eliot wrote after his religious conversion, is a meditation on the Biblical story of three wise men who visited the infant Jesus in Bethlehem, and on Lancelot

Andrewes' 1622 Nativity sermon about that story. Eliot told Conrad Aiken that he wrote *Journey of the Magi* "in three quarters of an hour after church time and before lunch one Sunday morning, with the assistance of half a bottle of Booth's gin."[38] This introduction suggests that he may have felt uncertain about the merit of the poem.

When asked what the new poem meant, Eliot explained simply enough: "I meant that the Magi were drawn by a power which they did not understand."[39] In his mind, *Journey of the Magi* posed a very specific question: "how fully was the Truth revealed to those who were inspired to recognise Our Lord so soon after the Nativity?"[40] That question implies additional queries: *Did the wise men apprehend the reality of the Catholic doctrine of the Incarnation? Did they understand that the infant child in front of them was, as later written in the Gospel of John, The Word made flesh?* Eliot, who had made an intellectual surrender to Catholic dogma but who remained a skeptic by nature, seems to be expressing doubt in the poem. *Journey* imagines that the wise men are tormented by a sudden awareness of a Truth they can't comprehend. According to the poet, one of Magi even yearns for death to "settle" his "indecision."[41]

Did Eliot himself share similar doubts at the time he wrote the poem? If so, he overcame them in the years that followed. In 1938 he wrote, "I take for granted that Christian revelation is the only full revelation; and that the fullness of Christian revelation resides in the essential fact of the Incarnation, in relation to which all Christian revelation is to be understood."[42] For the poet, the belief that Jesus Christ was the literal son of God was fundamental–and transformative. Robert Sencourt shared a telling anecdote about Eliot's response to someone who suggested that his Christianity was mere escapism. According to Sencourt, Eliot "explained that Christian faith, far from softening the edges of life, made each of them more cutting, because it gave a fuller and therefore more intense life; it also made life more poignant because it brought every issue of the soul into direct relation to Infinity; it made every obligation more pressing; at every turn, it demanded greater sacrifice and commitment."[43] On a related note, the poet reflected in a 1929 letter to Paul Elmer More, "It [is] rather trying to be supposed to have settled oneself in an easy chair, when one has just begun a long journey afoot."[44]

At the time of his conversion—and the composition of *Journey of the Magi*—Eliot's spiritual journey overwhelmed him. He was sustained by brief flashes of insight into the nature of his new life. In a September 1927 letter to his friend Geoffrey Faber, he wrote about a "sudden realization of being separated from all enjoyment, from all things of this earth, even from Hope; a sudden separation and isolation from everything; and at that same moment of illumination, a recognition of the fact that one can do without all these things, a joyful recognition of what John of the Cross means when he says that the soul cannot be possessed of the divine union until it has divested itself of the craving for all created beings."[45] Eliot was beginning to divest. In early 1928, he took a vow of celibacy and fully committed himself to a life of discipline and austerity.

Eliot's total commitment to the church transformed his poetry. In 1928 and 1929, he produced a sequence of fragments that would become *Ash-Wednesday*, his most distinctly Anglo-Catholic poem. In Western Christianity, Ash Wednesday refers to the first day of Lent, the liturgical season of reflection and penance leading up to Easter. Eliot's poem makes frequent allusions to Catholic rites, appropriating the language of Anglo-Catholic liturgy and invoking incantations from the late 16th and early 17th century—the literary high point of Anglo-Catholicism, as far as he was concerned.

Eliot also made use of the sermons of Lancelot Andrewes. One pivotal passage shows him scrutinizing every word in a particular sermon for deeper meaning, as he struggles to select the proper words to convey The Word. In 1926, Eliot had written about Andrewes' technique of taking a word and squeezing it until it yielded its "full juice of meaning."[46] Using a similar process, Eliot now crafted a new type of impersonal poetry, imbued with Biblical authority and meaning. *In Ash-Wednesday*, he squeezed the opening passage of the Gospel of John:

If the lost word is lost, if the spent word is spent
If the unheard, unspoken
Word is unspoken, unheard;
Still is the unspoken word, the Word unheard,
The Word without a word, the Word within
The world and for the world;
And the light shone in darkness and
Against the Word the unstilled world still whirled
About the centre of the silent Word.[47]

Ash-Wednesday is not, however, a completely impersonal poem. In a 1927 speech given before the Shakespeare Association, Eliot conceded that no poem could ever be completely impersonal, because "what every poet starts from is his own emotions." The goal, he said, is to get beyond those emotions, to "transmute his personal and private agonies into something rich and strange, something universal and impersonal."[48] Dante did this, he argued, through a combination of biography and allegory that has become alien to the modern mind; his work is visual "in the sense that he lived in an age in which men still saw visions."[49] By comparison, Eliot claimed, modern poets have only *dreams*, because people in the modern world have forgotten how to have *visions*. To properly experience Dante's work, then, he implored readers to shake off the modern preconception that Dante was writing allegories, and try to read his literary forays into hell, purgatory and paradise as visionary journeys–experiences that are every bit as real to the poet as dreams are real to the dreamer while the dreaming lasts.

Eliot theorized that what made Dante's visions especially real for Dante himself was a technique of basing his characters upon the people he knew in real life. He pointed to the character of Beatrice in the *Vita Nuova*, who was supposedly based on a young girl that Dante fell in love with as a child. In the *Vita Nuova*, Dante's poetry transforms Beatrice into an immortal symbol of love. In *The Divine Comedy*, she reappears as an angel who guides Dante's pilgrim from Purgatory to Paradise. In effect, Eliot wrote, Beatrice became Dante's "means of transition" from human love to divine love.[50] Drawing inspiration from the *Vita Nuova*, Eliot conceived *Ash-Wednesday* as "an exposition of my view on the relation of *eros* and *agape* based on my own experience."[51]

Like Dante, he may have had a real-life Beatrice. Biographer Lyndall Gordon points out that in 1927 Eliot reconnected with Emily Hale, the young Bostonian to whom he had declared his love in 1914. Although it is reductive to say that *Ash-Wednesday* is a poem about Eliot's relationship with Emily, Gordon suggests that the poem represents a stage in Eliot's spiritual autobiography, moving through Purgatory toward Paradise. Whether Hale served as the inspiration for *Ash-Wednesday* or not, it is certain that around this time, Eliot began writing that poem as an address to a mysterious "Lady." The earliest-written section of the poem contains a vision of three white leopards consuming the poet's vital organs, which is comparable to a scene in the *Vita Nuova* where Beatrice lovingly consumes Dante's heart. According to Eliot, this "Lady" came to him in a dream, along with some of the most enigmatic imagery in the poem. He chose to trust that vision, and use it as the foundation for his latest work. "The whole thing aims to be a modern *Vita Nuova*," he wrote in 1930, and "on the same plane of hallucination."[52]

Ultimately, the poet feared that his work fell pathetically short of Dante's model. Although the third section of *Ash-Wednesday* optimistically charts a symbolic ascent of Mount Purgatory (with instructive assistance from St. John of the Cross), the poet self-consciously fumbled with language in the later sections and failed to reach the Easter resurrection. Instead, he concluded the sequence with sea imagery reminiscent of his childhood summers, and a formal prayer for divine grace. This final plea is directed to another mysterious lady, the Virgin Mary—perhaps in the hope that she will serve as a "means of transition" from the time of tension to the promised land.

In a 1930 letter, the poet expressed disappointment with *Ash-Wednesday* as a whole, and advised one reader to wait for the "remote possibility" that a "Promised Land" that might appear in his poetry in another 10 or 15 years.[53] Having only just begun his long journey, he was humbly cautious about getting ahead of himself; he wanted to remain honest about the limitations of his own experience. In a 1932 essay, he elaborated, "We cannot make poetry out of what we should like to feel, nor can we summon up religious feelings for the purpose of writing religious verse. We can only use our strongest and deepest feelings, and we often do not know what those are."[54]

In hindsight, Eliot recognized the religious character of the feelings that inspired his early poetry. For that reason, he steadfastly refused to repudiate any of his early poems, instead, acknowledging them as honest expressions of earlier phases of the long spiritual journey. He clarified his perspective in a 1931 essay on Baudelaire, by characterizing the French poet's supposedly blasphemous poetry as essentially Christian, and insisting that Baudelaire was unconsciously occupied with "the real problem of good and evil."[55] He contextualized Baudelaire's work as an unconscious expression of Sin "in the permanently Christian sense," rather than an expression of sin "in the Swinburnian sense."[56] In his own "intermediate phase," Eliot was consciously confronting Sin in the permanently Christian sense, and praying for reconciliation. His intermediate poetry is a record of this season of personal reflection and penance.

In 1930, the second Ariel poem offered a faint, hopeful glimmer of Paradise ahead. The theme of *Marina*, Eliot told artist E. McKnight Kauffer, is paternity. The poem juxtaposes two moments of discovery: the Hercules of Seneca's *Hercules Furens* "waking up to find that he had slain his children" and Shakespeare's Pericles "waking up to find his child alive."[57] The contrast between life and death illuminates the projected final hour of Eliot's time of tension. Not coincidentally, the scenery in the poem is coastal New England, which seems to represent for Eliot an experience of wholeness: his present life informed by and infused with memories of his past, a spiritual death leading to a prospective rebirth. The poet would soon have a comparable full-circle experience in real life, as he returned to the America of his childhood—and to Emily Hale—during the autumn of 1932.

4. Four Quartets

After Strange Gods

In December 1931, Eliot was invited to Harvard University as a visiting professor for the upcoming academic year. He accepted the invitation at once, and began preparing his American lectures as an expression of his ideas about the current state of Western culture. At the same time, he was beginning to root his latest critical writings in the notion that all the problems of the modern world were ultimately religious. He wrote in a 1932 essay that the Western world was suffering from a "disorderly condition in which life seems to have lost all meaning and value," and argued that popular pseudo-religious ideologies like fascism and communism were struggling to fill a void that only religion could satisfy.[1] He also presented this belief in an unfinished play called *Coriolan*, about the rise of a diplomat. According to biographer Lyndall Gordon, the play was intended "to move from empty shows of power to a prophetic role and then on towards a state of mystical elevation based on St. John of the Cross."[2] *Coriolan* never progressed beyond politics—and that, in a way, illustrates Eliot's point. In 1931 he summed up, "The World is trying the experiment of attempting to form a civilized but non-Christian mentality. The experiment will fail." In the meantime, he said, it was the responsibility of genuine Christians to preserve the faith through the coming years so that it could be used eventually "to renew and rebuild civilization, to save the World from suicide."[3]

Eliot's Harvard lectures (published as *The Use of Poetry and the Use of Criticism*) mostly elaborated on earlier critical theories, but he tested his new ideas in a series of lectures delivered at the University of Virginia in the spring of 1933. His goal was to study contemporary literature as a moralist, and the Virginia lectures (published in 1934 as *After Strange Gods*) recast the old literary debate between classicism and romanticism as a distinction between religious orthodoxy and heresy. In the lectures, Eliot characterized James Joyce as "the most ethically orthodox of the more eminent writers of my time," and novelist D. H. Lawrence as the "perfect example of the heretic."[4] In an early written version of the final lecture, published in the *Virginia Quarterly Review*, he controversially declared Lawrence, and his 1928 novel *Lady Chatterley's Lover*, "spiritually sick."[5] Even more inflammatory was a remark he made in one of his lectures about the undesirability of "free-thinking Jews" in a culture aspiring to religious unity.[6] These comments contributed to a general perception that the newly-converted poet was a censorial bigot and a racist, and forced him to spend the rest of his life clarifying and defending his beliefs.

With regard to Eliot's moral judgment of literary peers, it is important to recognize that he did not advocate the censorship of literature, but instead consistently fought for freedom of expression. In the 1920s, he championed the literary merit of Joyce's sexually-explicit novel *Ulysses*, and defended it against accusations of obscenity in America. In September 1928, he joined E. M. Forster and Virginia Woolf in defending Radclyffe Hall's novel *The Well of Loneliness* against public discrimination. Eliot thought Hall's book dull and poorly written, but he argued that the author's good intentions should safeguard her work. A few months later, he joined Bernard Shaw and W. B. Yeats in defending William Joynson-Hicks' *The Prayer Book Crisis* against suppression by Irish Catholics. He summed up his position on censorship by writing that "the tyranny of religion is bad," and "the tyranny of 'morality,' with some wholly vague religious backing, or wholly divorced from any exact religion, is still worse."[7] His perspective remained virtually unchanged in 1960 when he was prepared to defend *Lady Chatterley's Lover* against legal obscenity charges in England—even though he remained ambiguous at best about the value Lawrence's work.

As a Christian, what Eliot objected to was heresy, which he defined in his UVA lectures as an insistence on partial truths or oversimplifications of truth. As a publisher and a social critic, however, he also strongly opposed tyranny in all its forms. Ironically, in the wake of the publication of *After Strange Gods*, he had to defend himself against accusations he was a fascist. Eliot had begun expressing an interest in fascism as a political philosophy in 1923, but by 1928 he had already become dismissive. To him, fascism and communism were not only poor substitutes for religion, but also flimsy alternatives to democracy. The latter criticism is more powerful when one realizes that Eliot was also openly critical of democracy. In a 1921 letter to English poet Richard Aldington, he wrote that he had a "profound hatred for democracy."[8] By the time he penned *The Idea of a Christian Society*, he had come to the belief that liberal democracy was little more than a window dressing for financial oligarchy. In the late 1920s, he stated his preference for the political philosophy of royalism, which to his mind was compatible with Catholicism—whereas fascism, communism, and unrestrained capitalism were practically atheistic or anti-religious. In the 1930s, however, the philosophy of royalism became increasingly aligned in the popular imagination with fascism, and Eliot spoke less frequently on the subject. After the end of World War II, he conceded that "democracy is the best form of society," but he remained critical of many democratic practices.[9]

The horrors of World War II also prompted Eliot to revisit his controversial comment about "free-thinking Jews," along with some unsavory-at-best lines in early poems (most notably, "Burbank with a Baedeker: Bleistein with a Cigar"), which had led to accusations of anti-Semitism. In a 1945 lecture at the Czecho-Slovak Institute in London, he declared, "I am not a supporter of any race doctrine, certainly of no philosophy of race superiority and inferiority in the modern sense. It is not blood that I am interested in, but the transmission of *culture*."[10] Two years later, he wrote emphatically in a private letter to poet Edward Field, "I am no more anti-Semitic than I am anti-Welsh or anti-Eskimo."[11] In a 1948 letter to literary critic Leslie G. Fielder, he tried to clarify that the offending line from *After Strange Gods* was "an expression of regret that so many Jews have lost their religious faith,"[12] and in a 1951 letter to Canon B.

Iddings Bell, he further suggested that reading the line as evidence of racial prejudice might be a product of "anti-anti-Semitic" zealotry.[13] In a 1959 interview, Eliot tried to definitively put the matter to rest by saying, simply, "I'm a Christian and therefore I'm not an anti-Semite."[14] For him, this was the final word on the matter, but the accusation of anti-Semitism continued to haunt him—and has haunted his legacy to such an extent that entire books have been written on the subject.

Eliot was obviously troubled by his own words in *After Strange Gods*. In later years, he told his friend Frederick Tomlin that although he thought the book had some "brilliant paragraphs," it was nevertheless "a bad book a bad book a bad book."[15] In 1962, he dismissed it outright as "an intemperate attack on the people with whom I disagree."[16] According to poet Donald Hall, he blamed the book on "a state of unhappiness which distorted his judgment" at the time.[17] And another poet, Stephen Spender, noted that Eliot went so far as to suggest that it was he, rather than D. H. Lawrence, who was "spiritually sick" in 1932.[18]

Certainly, Eliot was under a great deal of personal stress during his time in America. While there, he initiated legal proceedings to separate from his wife—a decision that had been at least five years in the making. He seems to have contemplated the possibility of remaining permanently in America and starting a new life with Emily Hale—a possibility that initially prompted feelings of youthful elation, embodied in his 1933 landscape poem "New Hampshire," but ultimately he dismissed the possibility of such a new beginning. For a time, he was in limbo. He wrote to a friend in England that he felt like Alice in Wonderland, looking at his life from the other side of the looking glass. "There is something I want here," he explained, pointing to the "domestic affection" he had found in America, "and something I want in England, and I can't have both; fortunately the time of choice is long since past."[19] In his final American lecture in 1933, Eliot seemed to be mentally preparing himself for his return to England. He said, "Most choices you can get over. I mean that if you make the wrong choice, you can rub it out and make another one, but there are always some choices sooner or later which are irrevocable and, whether you make the right one or the wrong one, there is no going back on it."[20] Although he would not be returning to Vivienne, Eliot remained committed to the life he had created for himself by marrying her in 1915. When he sailed home that summer, he had no clear idea of what his future would be.

Time Present

In June 1933, Eliot took up residence in rural Hereford parish, at the guesthouse of his friend and employer Frank Morley. According to Morley, life on Pikes Farm was "a ramshackle life, many things homespun, homemade, improvised," but he claimed that Eliot took to it immediately because the place had a "domesticity reminiscent in some ways of his own childhood."[21] In hindsight, the poet's time there looks like a trial run for the sort of monastic life he would lead for the remainder of the decade, but at the time Eliot was simply trying to figure out what came next. Within a matter of weeks, one way forward became apparent. He decided to focus on playwriting.

That fall, Eliot began work on *The Rock*, a religious revue intended to help raise money for the construction of 45 new churches in the suburbs of London. According to E. Martin Browne, the theater director who forged a creative alliance with the poet on the project and remained his collaborator for many years, Eliot approached *The Rock* as an opportunity to learn a new medium through practice and patience. He claimed that his main goal was to demonstrate a role for the Chorus in contemporary drama. Years later, Eliot reflected that he'd demonstrated a rather limited role; in his 1953 essay "The Three Voices of Poetry," he noted that the choral voice in *The Rock* was merely his poetic voice, "speaking *for me*, not uttering words that really represented any supposed character of their own."[22]

Today, *The Rock* is mainly remembered for Eliot's voice—his poetic ruminations on the conflict between the Church and the World, the Eternal and the Transient. Browne explained that Eliot's choral verses were stitched together using a then-popular theory of time expounded by British philosopher John William Dunne. In his 1927 book *An Experiment with Time*, Dunne presents dreamers and artists as time-travelers who are continually constructing present moments out of memories of the past and visions of the future. For Eliot, Dunne's theory of time might have echoed the philosophy of Henri Bergson, as well as his feeling (articulated in a 1917 letter to his mother) "that Time is not before and after, but all at once, present and future and all periods of the past."[23] This theory of time supported the unconventional narrative of *The Rock*, as Browne noted: "The scenes are not introduced in chronological order, but rather as they are called up by the experiences of 1934."[24] The printed program for the revue reads as follows: "*The Rock* is not a pageant in the usual sense. It does not consist of a number of historical scenes or tableaux in order of time. The aim is not merely to remind people that churches have been built in the past, but to employ the historical scenes to reinforce, in appropriate places, the emphasis upon the needs of the present."[25]

As a traditionalist, Eliot strongly valued historical knowledge and perspective. As an artist and a Christian, he also believed in values that are "realized only out of time."[26] The tension between these two points of view became the subject of Eliot's subsequent play. On the surface, *Murder in the Cathedral* is about a historical conflict between Church and State: the 1170 assassination of Thomas Becket, archbishop of Canterbury, during the reign of King Henry II. That piece of history resonated strongly during the time in which Eliot's play was written and performed, giving it a heightened effect on audiences. Theater owner Ashley Dukes later reflected that in June 1935, the month when *Murder in the Cathedral* premiered at the annual Canterbury Festival, "Hitler had been long enough in power to ensure that the four knightly murderers of Becket would be recognized as figures of the day, four perfect Nazis defending their acts on the most orthodox totalitarian grounds."[27]

Eliot, however, was not primarily concerned with the political implications of the play; what he wanted to examine was Becket's religious ascent. For the poet, the central action of the play was inner action–not the power struggle over Becket's physical life, but the turmoil of his spiritual life. In the play, each of the four Tempters tries to divert Becket from the path of righteousness by offering to spare his life if he will betray his religious convictions. Like Dante, Eliot based these figures on influential people from his own life and times. In private notes, he identified H. G. Wells, Bertrand Russell, D. H. Lawrence, Irving Babbitt, and either Julian or Aldous Huxley as character models.[28] For him, the important thing about these Tempters was their espousal of heretical ideas. Through Becket, Eliot was exploring his own struggle against the alluring but pernicious influence of heresy–overcoming the Tempters one by one in a kind of purification ritual. In the end, Becket becomes a martyr because he has surrendered his will completely in order to serve the will of God. His dying words sum up his achievement: "Now to Almighty God, to the Blessed Mary ever Virgin, to the blessed John the Baptist, the holy apostles Peter and Paul, to the blessed martyr Denys, and to all the Saints, I commend my cause and that of the Church."[29]

Eliot's work on *Murder in the Cathedral* also planted the seed for a four-part poem that would chart an ascent similar to that of Becket, while dispensing with the overtly Christian language that had defined much of the poet's work since 1927. The first segment of *Burnt Norton*, the beginning of Eliot's *Four Quartets*, grew out of a preliminary sketch written for the First Tempter, who aimed to seduce Becket with memories of the "leaping pleasure" of his comparatively libertine youth. In a 1953 interview, Eliot remembered, "There were lines and fragments that were discarded in the course of the production of *Murder in the Cathedral*. 'Can't get them over on the stage,' said the producer, and I humbly bowed to his judgment. However, these fragments stayed in my mind, and gradually I saw a poem shaping itself round them."[30]

Eliot told literary critic Helen Gardner that the inspirational fragments (posthumously published in *The Poems of T. S. Eliot* under the title "Bellegarde") "got mixed up" in his memory with lines from the beginning of Lewis Carroll's novel *Alice in Wonderland* and with personal memories of a visit to a secret garden at a house in the English countryside.[31] The poet probably visited Burnt Norton, a seemingly-abandoned manor house in the Cotswolds, in the summer of 1934 with his American friend Emily Hale, who was visiting relatives in the nearby town of Chipping Camden. The poet later wrote to Emily's relatives that they made him feel "at home [...] in a way in which I had not felt at home for some twenty-one years, anywhere."[32] This message—although written as a thank-you note, and thus perhaps exaggeratedly sentimental—suggests the possibility that he'd had an experience there reminding him of the leaping pleasures of his youth, before he left America, before Vivienne, before the war and the nervous breakdown that followed it.

Burnt Norton conveys an experience of hope and renewal, accompanied by a stark reminder that (to quote one of Eliot's early *Harvard Advocate* poems) time is time, and runs away. In the poem, the jubilant laughter of children is ghostly—merely an echo of the past. Bliss exists in the present moment, but it is followed by the pain of regret and remorse. This prevents the poet from succumbing to the temptation of emotional indulgence and disappearing permanently into the romantic fantasy of Wonderland.

For his own reasons, Eliot was convinced that he could not remain happy with Emily. *Burnt Norton* appears, at least partly, to reflect the couple's shared moment of summery bliss in an idyllic rose garden—but the moment soon gives way to a return to the dark night of the soul. For the time being, Eliot's spiritual autobiography remained in Purgatory.

Three Voices

1939 was a pivotal year for Eliot, as for the entire world. As Nazi

Germany invaded Poland and initiated World War II, the poet refocused his creative efforts by discontinuing his literary journal *The Criterion* and releasing three very different works. *The Family Reunion* was his first full-length play featuring modern characters in a contemporary setting, and it endures as one of his most personally revealing poetic works. *The Idea of a Christian Society*, a philosophical treatise on the future of Western civilization, was his first full-length book of social criticism. Finally, *Old Possum's Book of Practical* Cats, a collection of "nonsense verse," was unlike anything he had formally published before–a whimsical experiment in which words are used primarily for sonic effect. All these publications were the products of many years of trial and turmoil.

Old Possum's Book of Practical Cats had been germinating since at least 1931, when "Uncle Tom" began sending illustrated letters to his four-year-old godson Tom Faber, about the adventures of Pollicle Dogs and Jellicle Cats. Eliot's nonsense verses may have been inspired by memories of his father, who at some point illustrated a set of comic animals that his youngest son inherited. In 1931, Eliot apparently was resigned to the fact that he would never have any children of his own; he had taken a vow of celibacy in 1928, and even before that he had privately declared (to Bertrand Russell, of all people) that he would never have any heirs. In 1939, however, he confided to English critic John Hayward that he'd once had an acute desire to have children of his own. That desire seems to have been strongest during the years when he invented his own set of comic animals.

During those years, Eliot tested his children's verses on several private focus groups. He frequently visited the wife and three children of his friend George Tandy, and read the poems aloud to them. He later regaled the children of poet Michael Roberts and journalist Janet Adam Smith, who remembered Uncle Tom's routine as follows: "Book pressed into his hand, with some merriment; affected surprise; adjustment of spectacles; much turning to and fro of pages; renewed reluctance; increasing encouragement from audience–then, launched into Skimbleshankes, Growltiger or the

Rum-tum-tiger [sic], we were well away from another hour, Johnny sometimes on Tom's knee, especially when it came to his favorite Macavity."[33] In the spring of 1936, the Faber publishing house announced the forthcoming publication of *Mr. Eliot's Book of Pollicle Dogs and Jellicle Cats as Recited to Him by the Man in White Spats*—but soon after, Eliot told a friend that the project had been indefinitely delayed. He confessed that he was afraid of making a fool of himself by going public with a set of poems that was so different from the poetry he was known for. It would take several years for him to change his mind.

In the meantime, Eliot became preoccupied with poetic drama. In a 1937 speech, he said that his re-creation of medieval religious drama in *Murder in the Cathedral* seemed to him like a dead end, and asserted the need for modern poets to "reintegrate" religious and secular drama. Two years earlier, he had been even more pointed, saying, "What I want is a literature which should be *un*consciously, rather than deliberately and defiantly Christian."[34] His subsequent move away from distinctly Biblical language was a manifestation of the immutable belief that poetry is not about the assertion of any particular truth, but about "the making that truth more fully real to us [...] the making of the Word Flesh."[35] In *Ash-Wednesday*, *The Rock*, and *Murder and the Cathedral*, Eliot had relied heavily—but never exclusively—on the language of the King James Bible and Catholic liturgy; now he sought new voices to embody a universal wisdom.

In his 1953 essay "The Three Voices of Poetry," the poet explained that until 1938, his work had been "of the poet talking to himself" and "the poet addressing an audience."[36] In 1938, he discovered what he called the third voice of poetry, the voice of dramatic characters speaking in a language entirely their own. The first examples of this new voice appeared in *The Family Reunion*, a drawing-room comedy about an English aristocratic family haunted by one man's metaphysical dread. Eliot explained that his goal was "not to transport the audience into some imaginary world totally unlike its own," but to illuminate and transfigure their "sordid, dreary daily world," by creating distinctly individual characters and illuminating the world of those characters.[37] With that in mind, he introduced the Greek myth of the Furies—demons to some, angels to others—into the everyday lives of modern audiences.

Loosely based on *The Orestia* of Aeschylus, *The Family Reunion* was also partly derived from Eliot's personal experience. In a March 1938 letter to E. Martin Browne, the poet described the first completed draft of his play in terms that were clearly autobiographical. According to the letter, the main character in the play, Harry Monchesey, is recovering from a failed marriage that has left him "partially desexed." The character of Mary stimulates feelings of love (though *not* lust) in him for the first time since his marriage, and offers a new beginning that Harry eventually rejects in favor of a monastic life. Eliot elaborated, "This attraction glimmers for a moment in his mind, half-consciously as a possible 'way of escape,'" and prompts a divine intervention, but then the Furies instruct Harry that "the only way out is the way of purgation and holiness."[38] The religious implications of the story are wrapped up in a murder mystery, revolving around Harry's fear that he has murdered his wife. He was present when she disappeared from the deck of an ocean liner—but did he push her? Even Harry doesn't seem to know for sure, but he is wracked by guilt.

A newly published letter suggests that this scenario may have been inspired by a real-life experience. Eliot wrote to a friend that on his voyage to America in 1932, when he was contemplating a permanent separation from his wife and planning a reunion with Emily Hale, he met a young lady who asked him to "walk around the Deck with her as it was Dark & Slippery and she was afraid of Falling over Board." He walked alongside her for 20 minutes, at which point the young lady said she was going inside because being with him didn't provide her with "any feeling of Support."[39] Did this experience consciously or subconsciously inspire the plight of Harry Monchesey? We can only imagine—but it seems safe to assume that there is a great deal of Eliot in the character, and that his decision to leave his wife in 1933 was something of an inspiration. In *The Family Reunion*, the question of whether or not

Harry physically murdered his wife is ultimately irrelevant; the main subject of the play is Harry's need for expiation—because the character undeniably wanted to get rid of his wife, and at the very least committed an act of murder in his own imagination. For the author, it was a story about the state of a man's soul.

The poet's friend Frederick Tomlin recalled that Eliot once shocked him by saying that "if one had ever felt like 'murdering someone,' one could never do anything about it. Something had been registered in the past and in one's own being, and that was that."[40] If Eliot ever contemplated murdering his own wife, that too is beside the point. What is relevant is his belief that he effectively ended her life by leaving her. For several years after he requested a deed of separation in 1933, Vivienne searched for her husband throughout London—showing up at his workplace, continually harassing friends for information as to his whereabouts, and even trying to address him directly through ads in the classified section of a local paper—but she was chasing a ghost; he would not see her or talk to her. The couple had one more brief encounter, at a book signing, in November 1935; he made a hasty escape, and she never saw him again. After that, Vivienne became increasingly delusional. In July 1938, she was discovered wandering the streets of London at 5 o'clock in the morning, speaking in a "confused and unintelligible manner."[41] She was committed to a halfway house in Hampstead, where she would spend the rest of her life.

For Eliot, the guilt-inducing shock of Vivienne's incarceration was followed by an even bigger shock. In September, British prime minister Neville Chamberlain signed a nonaggression pact with German chancellor Adolf Hitler, surrendering Czechoslovakia to the Nazis. Like many of his fellow countrymen, Eliot was overwhelmed by "a feeling of humiliation, which seemed to demand an act of personal contrition, of humility, repentance, and amendment."[42] He saw the pact as incontrovertible evidence that Western civilization had become morally hollow at the core, and was about to end with a whimper. Eliot's sense of despair over this event contributed to his decision the following year to discontinue *The Criterion*; he believed that the journal had utterly failed in its goal of fortifying European culture against political fanaticism. In the final months before World War II, he decided to focus his energy on a series of lectures that would become the basis for his book *The Idea of a Christian Society*, a plea for the conscious maintenance of Christian culture during Europe's dark days ahead.

Eliot was not a pacifist, but he was extremely dubious about the causes of the impending war. His "idea for a Christian society" was not a call for theocracy, but a plea for common standards of moral instruction and an increased emphasis on education in the arts. In 1934, he had argued that the British education system should be "rearranged by people with some definite social philosophy and some notion of the true vocation of man," and now he boldly declared that only a "proper" system of education could unify the life of the nation, and rebuild Europe as a whole.[43] For Eliot, the ideal system of education would aim to instill a Christian philosophy of life–not necessarily turning students into faithful Christians, but helping them to think like ideal Christians, to be intellectually and morally disciplined. With that in mind, he promoted the notion of a national church as a unifying force for Christians and non-Christians alike.

The poet's prescription was eclipsed by the chaos of the day. *The Idea of a Christian Society* was published in October 1939. By then, Britain was at war with Germany, and the nation was mobilizing for its physical survival. A few months later, Eliot acknowledged that he had very little hope of stimulating immediate social change, but he resolved to continue promoting Christian values amidst the horrors of World War II.

War Quartets

In a 1959 interview, Eliot said that if the war hadn't happened, he would have gone to work on another play immediately after *The*

Family Reunion. Instead, he turned his attention back to poetry—in particular, to the four-part, five-movement form he had used in *Burnt Norton*. Eliot was experimenting with the form of a musical quartet, a classical composition utilizing four instruments or voices. In a 1931 letter, he told Stephen Spender that he had always admired Beethoven's late string quartets, which to his mind expressed "the fruit of reconciliation of relief after immense suffering," and that he hoped to get something similar "into verse before I die."[44] In a 1933 lecture at Yale University, he elaborated on this, saying that he wanted to get "*beyond poetry*, as Beethoven, in his later works, strove to get *beyond music*."[45] His words echoed a 1927 biography of Beethoven by author J. W. Sullivan, who declared that the German composer's late string quartets have a mystical quality expressing his deepest experiences of suffering and transcendence, and show him "exploring a new region of consciousness."[46] In the 1942 essay "The Music of Poetry," Eliot wrote that he likewise wanted to explore "frontiers of consciousness beyond which words fail, though meanings still exist."[47]

In the early days of the war, the poet found that he could only focus on poetry in short intervals of time. Luckily, he found that the quartet form suited those working conditions. He told interviewer Donald Hall, "I could write them in sections and [...] it didn't matter if a day or two elapsed when I did not write, as they frequently did, while I did war jobs."[48] The disjointed process of composition helped him to realize the form's "possibilities of contrapuntal arrangement of subject-matter."[49] He suggested to John Hayward that by weaving together several disparate themes into an "emotional whole," he could prompt readers to experience the poem *as a whole*—and to look for meaning beyond any particular phrase or set of phrases.[50] As he continued the experiment, Eliot began to acquire his own sense of the whole. He viewed *East Coker*, the first wartime quartet, not merely as a complement to *Burnt Norton* but also as a part of a projected sequence of four quartets, unified by "the symbolism of the four seasons and the four elements."[51]

East Coker, he decided, would represent the element of earth and the season of summer, drawing inspiration from one summer day in particular. In June 1936, and again in August 1937, the poet visited the rural English village of West Coker. On the latter trip, he took a slow walk to the 13th-century church of St. Michael in East Coker. The poet knew that his Eliot ancestors had lived in East Coker from the mid-15th century until the late 17th century, so for him, it was a return to his ancestral home. With that in mind, he decided to use East Coker as a poetic point of departure, "a place for a meditation on beginnings and ends."[52] Although he wrote the poem with that specific village in mind, he maintained that many other places could have served the purpose just as well. His theme was not exclusively personal; it was also national and universal.

In early 1940, when Eliot completed *East Coker*, England was braced for war. In April, the Nazis invaded Norway. Three months after that, the Battle of Britain began. From that point on, Londoners had to live with the constant threat of aerial bombings. For Eliot, the lulling heat and peace of that day in August 1937 must have seemed like a distant memory. The intention of his poem, however, was not to evoke warm, sunny nostalgia; he wanted to juxtapose past and present, war and peace, in such a way that the poem would inspire much more than sentimental reflection. One of the ways he did this was by contrasting the oppressive urban atmosphere that had dominated his earlier poetry with the comparatively serene landscapes of his more recent work (not to mention some of England's best-known Romantic poetry). In *East Coker*, the landscapes exist not as distinct places, but as separate aspects of an experience with no clear beginning or end. The poem thus became a meditation on non-dualism in the mystical night of the soul:

> I said to my soul, be still, and wait without hope
> For hope would be hope for the wrong thing; wait without love
> For love would be love of the wrong thing; there is yet faith
> But the faith and the love and the hope are all in the waiting.
> Wait without thought, for you are not ready for thought:
> So the darkness shall be the light, and the stillness the dancing.[53]

Eliot continued this spiritual pilgrimage in his third quartet, *The Dry Salvages*, which begins far from war-torn Europe. The title harkens back to the poet's childhood summers in coastal New England, signifying a navigational landmark off the eastern corner of Cape Ann, Massachusetts. For Eliot, it was one of many landscape symbols taken from his unwritten memoir *The River and the Sea*, and it evoked many ideas, both personal and impersonal. *The Dry Salvages* charts the poet's journey to the east, from the banks of the Mississippi River all the way to St. Michael's Church in East Coker, from the poet's "beginning" in St. Louis to the place where his ashes would be interred after his death. This personal voyage runs parallel to a spiritual journey to the East, as the poem intermingles symbols and concepts from Western philosophy and religion with symbols and concepts from Hinduism and Buddhism.

The central movement of the poem invokes an exchange from the sacred Hindu text *The Bhagavad Gita*, between the soldier Arjuna and the god Krishna, about the morality of war. Arjuna, a soldier pitted against some of his own family members, questions the righteousness of continuing to fight. Krishna instills in him a sense of detachment from the outcome of his actions, and an even greater sense of duty to divine forces beyond his comprehension. In the midst of war, this notion of surrender to a higher power—one that is both creative and destructive in ways that human beings cannot fathom—apparently resonated with Eliot. He himself was a witness to the ravages of war; in the autumn of 1940, he volunteered as an air-raid warden in the Kensington district of London during the Blitz, and was responsible for corralling his neighbors in an underground train station during attacks. Later, he became a firewatcher in Bloomsbury, and spent several nights each week on the roof of the Faber & Faber office in Russell Square, watching and waiting. When he wasn't performing these "war jobs," he stayed with friends outside of the city, and struggled—through his writing—to express a sense of order amid chaos. In November, he wrote to his secretary, "Unless I can produce some work of value this winter, I shall not feel justified in this life."[54]

The Dry Salvages was published in February 1941, at the height of air raids on London. At that time, the future of England seemed grim. A month later, Eliot's friend Virginia Woolf—who he regarded as practically family, and also the hub of the literary world in London—committed suicide. Around the same time, Eliot wrote a eulogy for his friend and esteemed peer James Joyce, who had died in January. He also recently had given a memorial lecture on the late W. B. Yeats, praising him as the 20th-century poet most worthy of emulation. Eliot felt that he was fighting against the crushing tide of time, struggling to produce a literary work that could "redeem the time."

In the fall of 1941, as he struggled to complete his fourth quartet, Eliot worried that he was rushing his work, "trying to make poetry out of unseasoned material."[55] Initially, he believed that *Little Gidding* was defective due to "the lack of some acute personal reminiscence" equivalent to the points of departure in his earlier quartets.[56] Like the other poems, *Little Gidding* was inspired by a particular landscape—in this case, a rural parish near Cambridge that the poet had visited in the spring of 1936. Unlike the other poems, however, *Little Gidding* was not exclusively inspired by Eliot's own impressions of the place. He also built this work upon second-hand impressions.

Eliot's sense of Little Gidding was heavily influenced by J. Henry Shorthouse's 1881 novel *John Inglesant*, which depicts the monastic-like community of Little Gidding, and the historic chapel at the heart of that community, as a point of convergence for a certain type of literary classicism, royalism, and Anglicanism. During the Jacobean era, Little Gidding was home to the family of Nicholas Ferrar, a devout Anglican and close friend of metaphysical poets George Herbert and Richard Crashaw. During the English Civil War, Ferrar had acted as a faithful loyalist, sheltering the dethroned King Charles I near his home on the night of May 2, 1646, while republican soldiers sought to arrest him. Afterward, the soldiers allegedly ransacked the church as punishment for Ferrar's allegiance to the King, forcing the community of Little Gidding to rebuild. Two centuries later, Shorthouse's novel revisited the legend, revived interest in 17th-century Anglicanism and the metaphysical poets, and delivered a ready-made symbol to Eliot, who—as a royalist—was deeply affected by the story.

In the fourth quartet, Eliot presents Little Gidding as an "intersection" of time and "the timeless moment," an enduring symbol of transcendence. In his mind, it was a place that had known war and had served as a refuge from war; had been devastated by war, but not permanently destroyed by it. In Eliot's time—and still today—the church at Little Gidding remained a sacred place of worship, where the eternal message of the King of Kings could put any earthly war into a larger perspective. For Eliot, the poem itself similarly placed the experience of World War II into a larger context, by juxtaposing imagery of war-torn modern London with historical examples of transcendent poetry and mystical experience. The supra-personal voice of the poem is a "familiar compound ghost" containing the voices of many predecessors—including Edgar Allan Poe, Percy Bysshe Shelley, Stéphane Mallarmé, W. B. Yeats, Shakespeare, John Milton, and Dante. Eliot wrestled with the words of these literary frontiersmen in an attempt to help preserve a particular literary tradition, and also to help expand the consciousness of modern readers beyond their own historical milieu.

In the final movement of *Little Gidding*, Dante gives way to St. John of the Cross, Dame Julian of Norwich, and the anonymous author of *The Cloud of Unknowing*. Eliot explained to John Hayward that he drew on the work of these three 14th-century mystics because he was worried about over-romanticizing 17th-century writers, and wanted to "give greater historical depth to the poem by allusions to the other great period" of English metaphysical literature—thereby illuminating the timeless moment that is Now.[57] On this ever-present frontier of consciousness—where words fail, though meanings persist—Eliot concluded his war with language, and surrendered his poetic voice to the mysteries of God.

Four Quartets was published as a completed sequence for the first time in 1943. On one level, the sequence is a deeply personal expression of Eliot's Anglo-Catholic faith. Like *The Waste Land*, however, it is also a meditation on civilization. The most astute readers and critics immediately recognized the sequence as a culmination of the poet's work—not merely a continuation of his increasingly extra-literary work of the 1930s, but the assimilation of everything that had come before it. The sequence encapsulates Eliot's entire supra-personal journey through St. Louis, Boston, London, American Puritanism, English Romanticism, French Symbolism, Bergsonism, Bradleyism, Hinduism, Buddhism, marriage, separation, the Inferno, Purgatory, two world wars and (not to be overdramatic) some 3,000 years of words made flesh. Beethoven's biographer J. W. Sullivan wrote that in his late string quartets, the composer achieved a "final synthesis" of "the primary elements of his experience" by "abandoning nothing."[58] The same thing is true for Eliot, who used the same phrase years earlier. In his 1919 essay "Tradition and the Individual Talent," Eliot wrote that a poet "must be aware that the mind of Europe—the mind of his own country—a mind which he learns in time to be much more important than his own private mind—is a mind which changes, and that this change is a development which abandons nothing *en route*."[59] Eliot's work as a whole explores an even larger mind—inescapably American as well as Eastern—and strives to move beyond mind, into a new realm of consciousness.

As a result, *Four Quartets* speaks to a much wider and broader audience than Anglicans or even Christians. Stephen Spender believed that although Eliot was consciously dogmatic, his best poetry was essentially mystical, and therefore as much Buddhist (or Indian) as Christian. Some critics have gone further, pointing to the wide variety of ideas and symbolism in Eliot's work as evidence that the poet subscribed to a kind of perennial philosophy. In 1946, Eliot freely admitted that his poetry showed "the influence of Indian thought and sensibility" and fused "Eastern and Western currents of feeling," but he denied being a universalist, or even a Christian ecumenist.[60] As he clarified in 1951, "I am aware [...] that there are readers who persuade themselves that there is an 'essence' in all religions which is the same, and that this essence can be conveniently distilled and preserved, while every particular religion is rejected. Such readers may perhaps be reminded that no man has ever climbed to the higher stages of the spiritual life, who has not been a believer in a particular religion or at least a particular philosophy."[61]

In his early 60s, Eliot apparently no longer felt compelled to claim that any particular religion has exclusive access to truth, or to accuse anyone of heretical beliefs. He recognized that different religious principles hold a common value for those who believe in them, and also that there is a difference between belief and wisdom. "Of revealed religions, and of philosophical systems," he wrote, "we must believe that one is right and the others wrong. But wisdom is [...] the same for all men everywhere. If it were not so, what profit could a European gain from the Upanishads or the Buddhist Nikayas? Only some intellectual exercise, the satisfaction of a curiosity, or an interesting sensation like that of tasting some exotic oriental dish."[62] For Eliot, the study of different cultures and beliefs was certainly more than merely an exercise of intellectual curiosity. Throughout his life, he maintained that his early study of Eastern religions had been immensely valuable to him. In 1933, at a time when he seemed to be at his most ideologically inflexible, he declared that "some of the early Buddhist scriptures affect me as parts of the Old Testament do."[63] His final essay, published in 1962, included a statement that he was personally "very thankful for having had the opportunity to study the *Bhagavad Gita* and the religious and philosophical beliefs, so different from [my] own, with which the *Bhagavad Gita* is informed."[64] These studies were a vital influence on his poetry—and a vital part of his worldview, a lifelong attempt to balance wisdom and holiness.

Eliot remained a committed Anglo-Catholic for the rest of his life.

He also remained a committed poet—because, as he explained, "the language of poetry is the language most capable of communicating wisdom."[65] Although he only wrote a few minor poems in his later years, the *Four Quartets*—and *Little Gidding* in particular—stands as his ultimate poetic achievement. In a 1958 interview, he reflected, "I feel I reached the end of something with the *Four Quartets*, and that anything new will have to be expressed in a different idiom."[66] In private conversation with his friend William Turner Levy, he was even more emphatic: "I stand or fall on them."[67]

5. The Elder Statesman

Christianity and Culture

When World War II ended in 1945, Eliot was not entirely relieved. Europe's long process of rebuilding had begun, and the poet knew that this would require more effort than just reconstructing cities and economies. He believed that Western culture itself had become fractured, and that the survival of Europe now depended on a serious reevaluation of its religious foundation. According to Eliot's friend Robert Sencourt, "It was not simply a question of rebuilding the *status quo ante*, but of reformulating the forms, attitudes, and outlook of the Christian church for its mission in the latter half of the twentieth century."[1] In 1947, Eliot reflected that although the war had been "precipitated by Germany's repudiation of Europe, and Japan's repudiation of Asia," the two aggressors merely exposed "a malady with which the world was already infected."[2]

Eliot had diagnosed the "malady" before the war began, and started trying to formulate the challenges of postwar construction as early as 1938 when he joined a small group of British intellectuals called The Moot. Founded by Christian ecumenist J. H. Oldham, and inspired by the writings of German sociologist Karl Mannheim, The Moot was created to help formulate a "new Christendom." In one of the group's early meetings, Eliot himself spoke of "the necessity for the re-education of the people's sense of values," and expressed a desire for a new social order based on Christian ideals.[3] He did not, however, believe that The Moot should (or could) inaugurate any specific political or social program; instead, he argued that a new social consciousness would have to emerge gradually and organically—with members of The Moot providing encouragement in certain directions.

As the war wound down, The Moot lost momentum, and Eliot strove to articulate his view of the challenges ahead fully. The title of his 1948 book *Notes towards the Definition of Culture* illustrates the tentativeness of his ideas, as he struggled to formulate a precise definition of the word "culture." Eliot's friend Frederick Tomlin later commented that "in those days people tended to talk about 'civilization' rather than 'culture,'" taking for granted that "civilization or 'civilization as we know it' was what people had fought for," while culture was "associated with what the Germans had believed they had fought for."[4] Eliot, however, did not inherit the word "culture" from the Germans. He had begun using the term in the 1920s, in relation to the work of English poet and social critic Matthew Arnold, whose 1869 book *Culture and Anarchy* defined culture as "contact with the best which has been thought and said in the world."[5] After his religious conversion, Eliot began criticizing Arnold's implied definition of "the best." In 1930, he complained that "the total effect of Arnold's philosophy is to set up Culture in the place of Religion, and to leave Religion to be laid waste by the anarchy of feeling."[6] From Eliot's perspective, in contrast, religion must exist at the core of any significant and enduring culture.

In the first half of *Notes towards the Definition of Culture*, written during World War II, the poet's attempts to define the word "culture" continually drew him back to the conclusion that people's moral and spiritual life is a vital correlative to their intellectual and imaginative life. To deny this unity, he said, is to create a divided consciousness and hasten the disintegration of a cohesive culture. In 1944, the poet expressed hope that a meaningful association and ongoing dialogue among society's spiritual and intellectual elite might help to restore cultural unity. Naturally, he had distinct ideas about the role of artists in the mission. Eliot felt responsible personally for helping to revitalize the "Christian Imagination" in the modern age of divided consciousness, in which (he said) the arts are not adequately nourished by theology and philosophy. He also argued that all scholars—political, philosophical, artistic, and scientific—have a responsibility to disseminate cultural knowledge to those who do not have their educational advantages. In general, his critical emphasis—like that of so many British reformers after the war—was on education. Somewhat controversially, he believed that "education should help to preserve the class and select the elite." At the same time, he acknowledged that an education system designed to uphold class distinctions would be "unattainable in practice," inevitably leading to unfairness and disunity.[7] Upon reaching this impasse, Eliot turned to the celebration of family and neighbors as the primary transmitters of culture. Ideally, he wrote, these local influences instill an abiding sense of "piety towards the dead," "solicitude for the unborn," "interest in the past" and "responsibility for the future."[8]

The second half of *Notes towards the Definition of Culture*, written after the war ended, focuses on the state of the European Union. Eliot was a vocal supporter of UNESCO, a United Nations agency dedicated to promoting international collaboration in the fields of culture, science, and education, and an outspoken critic of postwar mass deportations. He did not believe that Germans living in England should be punished for their nationality, and instead argued that Brits and Germans alike should be encouraged to renew their common bond as Europeans. In a postwar radio broadcast on the BBC in Germany, he publicly pleaded for "variety in unity," saying, "An error of the Germany of Hitler was to assume that every other culture than that of Germany was either decadent or barbaric. Let us have an end of such assumptions."[9] In subsequent years, he continued to excoriate excessive nationalism, while calling for a Christian culture in which all subcultures would be "variants," and all people would help to conserve and nourish the spiritual life of Europe.[10]

Eliot advocated a particular role for poets and men of letters in the cultural restoration of Europe. Echoing an important passage in *Little Gidding*, he frequently reiterated his belief that it was the poet's responsibility to help "purify the dialect of the tribe." For him, that meant preserving language from cultural chaos, as well as extending and improving it, and thereby expanding the consciousness of the people who use it. In his 1945 essay "The Social Function of Poetry," he clarified, "So far as he expresses, in his poetry, what other people feel, he is also affecting that feeling by making it more conscious: in giving people words for their feelings, he is teaching them something about themselves. But he is not merely more conscious than others; he is also different from them, and different from other poets, and can therefore give his readers knowledge of feelings which they have never experienced."[11] In later lectures, he emphasized the poet's responsibility to language as the ultimate medium for wisdom. He also stressed, and fulfilled, a publisher's responsibility to society—by curating the work of the best contemporary poets he could find, from Dylan Thomas to W. H. Auden. For Eliot, these were sacred duties that he faithfully carried out until his death.

Death and Rebirth

During the postwar years, as Eliot became an unofficial ambassador of international cultural diplomacy, he simultaneously withdrew into a private world. From 1946 until 1957, he shared a quiet flat in Chelsea with his friend John Hayward, who acted as a constant literary advisor, a social guardian, and (if Hayward is to be believed) a private confessor. While there, the poet's daily routine was simple and rote. He woke up early to attend morning mass at St. Stephen's Church on Gloucester Road, then returned to his flat for breakfast, and wrote there for several hours. Around noon, he traveled by bus and train to the offices of Faber & Faber in Russell Square, where he wrote promotional materials and performed regular duties as a creative director of the firm. At 4 pm, he ritualistically took his tea and received visitors. After the office closed, he sometimes attended social and literary functions, playing the obligatory role of elder statesman. The rest of the time, he returned home via taxi, ate dinner alone, and retired to his room–a spartan hovel with nicotine-stained walls.

Eliot's withdrawal into this private world began in 1947 when two personal events jolted him into what he purportedly described as a "psychological change of life."[12] The first event was the sudden death of Vivienne Eliot. Because she supposedly had been in good physical health, the news came as a genuine shock to Eliot and left him feeling "disintegrated."[13] On a cold day in January, he attended his wife's funeral in a bombed-out rural church. Friends Geoffrey and Enid Faber, who accompanied him, remembered it as "a rather trying ceremony."[14]

Eliot's shock over his wife's death was compounded by a second tragedy a few months later. In late April, he sailed to Boston to visit his brother Henry. Within a few days of his arrival in the U.S., Henry died of leukemia. Afterward, Henry's widow Theresa naively tried to turn the solemn occasion into a happy one–by offering to help plan a wedding for him and Emily Hale. According to Theresa's friend, Eliot responded to the offer with "white fury."[15] He later explained that, when Vivienne died, "I realised quite suddenly that I was deluding myself with emotions I had felt in the past, that I had changed more, and in ways unsuspected, than I had thought."[16]

In May 1947, he told Emily Hale that his feelings toward her had changed. She reportedly accepted his explanation and promised not to press the subject of marriage–but did not completely give up hope that he might one day "recover from this–to me–abnormal reaction."[17] For his part, Eliot sensed that the "psychological change of life" was permanent; he believed that he had fully depleted his emotional vitality. In a sense, it seems that he felt like his life was over. A few weeks later, he gave a despairing lecture at Concord Academy in Massachusetts, in which he expressed fear that nothing he had ever written had "permanent value" and he would "never again write anything good."[18] Stephen Spender recalls visiting Eliot after his return to London and finding him playing solitaire in his room. When Spender asked why he liked the game, Eliot responded, "Well, I suppose it's because it's the nearest thing to being dead."[19]

The poet expressed equally morbid sentiments in late 1948 when he was awarded the Nobel Prize in Literature. Publically, he accepted the award as "an assertion of the supra-national value of poetry," and embraced his role as "a symbol, for a time, of the significance of poetry."[20] Privately, he told poet John Berryman that he regarded the accolade as a "ticket to one's own funeral," because "no one has ever done anything after he got it."[21] The fame that accompanied the award made him feel ghostly, as he explained to an American interviewer in 1948. "One seems to become a myth," he said, "a fabulous creature that doesn't exist."[22] Poet John Malcolm Brinnin observed that, during this time, celebrity-hunters began following Eliot to church, requiring him "to live up to an image he could not live down."[23] The publication of a book of tribute essays on the occasion of his 60th birthday probably did not help; several of the essays read as if they were eulogies.

One of the few people who got close to Eliot during these later years was Mary Trevelyan, a London-based teacher and humanitarian missionary. The two first met at a fundraiser in 1938, and in 1940 began a lengthy correspondence that lasted through the war (and became the basis for Trevelyan's 1946 memoir *I'll Walk Beside You*). When the war was over, they became social companions, and Trevelyan—like the unfortunate Emily Hale—fell in love with the emotionally-unavailable poet. In 1949, when Eliot complained to her that his newfound celebrity was a "most desperately lonely business," she recommended a practical solution: marriage. Eliot turned down the proposal, telling her that he was "burnt out."[24] She tried the following year again, and he offered a slightly more elaborate excuse, making vague allusions to his failed relationship with Emily Hale. Trevelyan concluded, "All genius is, by its very nature, selfish."[25]

Despite his claims about being burnt out, Eliot was becoming creatively restless again. In 1948, he started working on a new play. His long-time collaborator E. Martin Browne remarked that, at least in terms of his literary life, Eliot was "determined to go on growing."[26] The poet said as much himself in a 1953 interview: "It has always struck me as very odd the way some poets–Browning for instance–have gone on writing in their old age without taking any step forward or making any new discovery. Why go on and on doing what you've already done well? I myself want each poem or group of poems to be different, a separate creation."[27] Determined to overcome the weaknesses he perceived in *The Family Reunion*, the poet sought to discipline his poetry–to put it "on a very thin diet"[28]–for the sake of dramatic utility. He resolved that in his new play, a romantic comedy entitled *The Cocktail Party*, he would put less emphasis on ideas and more emphasis on characterization. The decision displeased some of his critics, but the play was nevertheless a major commercial success, further enhancing the poet's fame and granting him financial security for the first time in his life.

Just as the work of Aristophanes and Aeschylus inspired Eliot's earlier plays, *Sweeney Agonistes* and *The Family Reunion*, so *The Cocktail Party* drew some inspiration from the classical writings of Euripides. Eliot explained to an interviewer in 1953 that the story of Edward and Lavinia Chamberlayne, whose troubled marriage is revitalized by an illusion of the wife's death, was a kind of extrapolation from the ending of Euripides' play *Alcestis*. That play ends with a promise that Alcestis, the wife of Heracles, will rise from the dead in three days–but, Eliot wondered, what would happen then? Using this question as a point of departure, he invented the character of Celia Coplestone, Edward's mistress, to "throw light on the relationship between the man and his wife," and then created the character of Sir Henry Harcourt-Reilly, to perform the god-like feats of Heracles that bring the couple back together.[29]

As Eliot continued to write, the character of Celia became increasingly important. In a July 1948 letter to the playwright, collaborator E. Martin Browne opined that she was "the character whom above all we want to love–the heroine, the play's necessary focus of sympathy."[30] Eliot had already begun to think of Celia as a correlative to Harry Monchesey, the central figure in his earlier play, *The Family Reunion*. He wrote to Browne that he didn't want to "leave her in the air like Harry."[31] Celia's fate—juxtaposed with the fate of Edward and Lavinia—represents a new stage in the spiritual journey that Eliot had been charting in his work for years. Stephen Spender offered this summation: "The theme is a recapitulation of his preoccupations of the last twenty-four years, from the nihilism of *Sweeney Agonistes* to the faith of *Four Quartets*."[32] The finished play illustrates two paths toward salvation—one solitary, and one beginning with a profound acknowledgment of the shared human experience of solitude and isolation. The god-like character of Sir Henry Harcourt-Reilly advises the living (including us, as audience members) to choose a path, and "work out your salvation with diligence."[33] Eliot was trying to work out his own salvation.

Mary Trevelyan's *The Pope of Russell Square: A Memoir of T. S. Eliot* (still unpublished as of 2018 but extensively quoted in Lyndall Gordon's *The Imperfect Life of T. S. Eliot*, and in Carole Seymour-Jones's a biography of Vivienne Eliot) paints a harrowing portrait of the poet in the postwar years. Quotations from this memoir suggest that the man she knew had much more in common with the tormented character of Harry Monchesey—still haunted by the Furies—than with the staid and self-assured Sir Harcourt-Reilly. According to Trevelyan, Eliot suffered from recurring nightmares in which he was punished for the murder of his wife, and from auditory hallucinations, in which male and female voices taunted him. At times, Trevelyan reportedly witnessed the poet becoming enraged or hysterical, for no reason that she could discern.

In November 1953, at a football stadium in Minnesota where he lectured to a record-breaking crowd of nearly 14,000 people, Eliot spoke candidly about the oppressive life of a poet, saying, "He is haunted by a demon, [...] and the words, the poem he makes, are a kind of form of exorcism of this demon."[34] Eliot was speaking figuratively, but perhaps also confessionally, as he described an intense yearning for "relief from acute discomfort," and an experience of "something very near annihilation, which is in itself indescribable."[35]

By the time he gave this lecture, Eliot had already completed his next play, a drawing room comedy entitled *The Confidential Clerk.* Using Euripides' *Ion* as a point of departure, this work echoes the paternal theme of Eliot's poem *Marina*, as well as the striving in *Four Quartets* for peace beyond words. The story begins with a wealthy businessman named Claude Mulhammer, and his relationship with a young clerk and aspiring musician named Colby Simpkins, who Mulhammer mistakenly believes to be his illegitimate son. A series of events unravels several cases of mistaken identity, and ultimately reunites Mulhammer with his actual child: a daughter named Lucasta. Colby's story, however, remains central to the play, helping to convey its theme of transcendence. The young musician concludes that he is quite simply a child of God, and that making music is, for him, like unlocking a door to the sort of Edenic garden described in *Burnt Norton*.

For Eliot, the play's profundity was related to the communicative directness of music, which he tried to convey through simple storytelling and simple language. He reportedly told his friend William Turner Levy that *The Confidential Clerk* was "less complicated" than *The Cocktail Party*, but had "more in layers to be meditated on and thought of as meanings of life."[36] For most of his own life, Eliot had been aiming at that kind of simplicity. In 1919 he wrote, "Great simplicity is only won by an intense moment or by years of intelligent effort, or by both. It represents one of the most arduous conquests of the human spirit: the triumph of feeling and thought over the natural sin of language."[37] In the mid-1930s, he speculated that such simplicity might eventually come through "a gradual mastery of one's emotions,"[38] arriving later in life, after many years of effort and discipline.

By the mid-1950s, he sensed that he was running out of time for such an achievement. According to Levy, a serious heart attack in April 1953 prompted Eliot to declare that "one must not try to do so many things, or *waste* any of the time that is left—and that one must husband one's strength for the things that matter most."[39] Despite his stubborn insistence on achieving his goals independently, he would—mercifully—not have to go the rest of the way alone.

Valerie

In 1940, a young English girl named Valerie Fletcher heard actor John Gielgud read Eliot's poem *Journey of the Magi*. For her, the experience was revelatory, and she became convinced that she "had to get to Tom, to work with him."[40] In 1950, when Valerie was 24 years old, she became Eliot's personal secretary at Faber & Faber. Throughout the following decade, she proved her loyalty time and time again, and her responsibilities increased as the sexagenarian poet's health declined. In May 1956, Eliot's flat-mate John Hayward, who suffered from multiple sclerosis, observed, "It's rapidly becoming apparent that he needs a nurse more than I do. And I have an informed suspicion that the ever-adoring Miss Fletcher is ready to assume the role."[41]

Later that year, Margaret Behrens—a mutual friend of Eliot and his adoring secretary—helped to facilitate a much more intimate relationship. Valerie remembered, "She wrote to him and said: 'Look, why don't you come out for the winter. Valerie can stay with me, and you can go to the hotel next door, it'll be fine.' Tom wrote back and said: 'I can't: I'm in love with her.' So Margaret wrote back and said: 'Get on with it.' And she wrote straight to me, too, and told me, then wrote back to him again and said: 'Good heavens, don't you realise she's in love with you?'"[42] Soon after, Eliot slipped a written marriage proposal into a batch of letters that his secretary was typing up for him. They married in secret on January 10, 1957.

Not everyone was happy for the newlyweds. When Eliot abruptly vacated the flat he had shared with John Hayward since 1946, the ex-roommate reportedly began referring to himself as the widow. When Emily Hale learned about the marriage, a friend claimed that she "nearly went out of her mind."[43] As for Mary Trevelyan, her nephew claimed that "she never recovered from the shock of Eliot's marriage, and spent a great deal of the remainder of her life mulling over what had happened."[44]

In sharp contrast to the emotional wreckage of these abandoned intimacies, many of Eliot's friends observed that the marriage profoundly transformed the poet for the better. One such friend, Frederick Tomlin, wrote that it seemed "as if a great weight had been lifted from his shoulders," and added, "He recovered almost boyish spirits, and his later years were the idyll that most people experience, if at all, in the first flush of youth."[45] Author Joseph Chiari concurred, "He was like a child who rediscovers the dear being he had lost, and who from then on feels protected against all possible aggressions in life, and even against death."[46] In 1959, Donald Hall offered the following portraits of his friend before and after: "At the age of sixty-two or -three, he had been pale, stooped, and cadaverous, with a hacking cough; now at the age of seventy–but with a new young wife [...] he looked debonair, sophisticated, lean, and handsome, with a fine tan just acquired in the Caribbean."[47] The Eliot who in 1927 saw a void in the middle of all human relations had apparently been converted.

The transformation is chronicled in Eliot's final play, *The Elder Statesman*. The first act, which Eliot began writing in 1956, revolves around the character of Lord Claverton, described by director E. Martin Browne as "a hallow man, who wears a 'public mask, under which he fears that there is no identity." The first draft of the play, Browne wrote, was about this character's "daring to strip off the mask, to find the identity."[48] Later, around the time that Eliot professed his love to Valerie, the focus shifted toward Lord Claverton's daughter Monica, and her lover Charles. The third act, written after Eliot's secret marriage, gave stronger voices to the young lovers. In one strikingly effusive passage, Charles boldly declares his feelings for Monica: "Oh my dear, / I love you to the limits of speech, and beyond. / It's strange that words are so inadequate. / Yet, like the asthmatic struggling for breath, / So the lover must struggle for words."[49]

Like a young lover himself, Eliot struggled to find the proper words to express his feelings for Valerie. His attempts include "To My Wife," the final poem published during the poet's lifetime, and a series of uncharacteristically erotic poems that were published for the first time in 2015. The latter are not solemn Dantescan prayers to an idealized Beatrice, but rapturous celebrations of earthly, flesh-and-blood union, and they suggest that Eliot was finally able to move—in life, if not in art—beyond words.

Martin Browne, reflecting on the love poetry in the final act of *The Elder Statesman*, suggested in 1969 that his friend had distilled "the essence of fresh love in a fashion reminiscent of *The Tempest*."[50] With that suggestion in mind, one is tempted to consider Eliot's final vision of Paradise as Shakespearean rather than Dantescan. In 1929, the poet wrote that Dante's body of work "is one of those which one can only just hope to grow up to at the end of life."[51] In 1962, he proclaimed that "a lifetime is hardly enough for growing up to" Shakespeare.[52] In the intervening years, he defined the ideal verse-drama as a perfect marriage of "dramatic and musical order," and suggested that Shakespeare had achieved this effect in his later plays.[53] No doubt he was thinking specifically of works he had repeatedly championed in his literary criticism: *Antony and Cleopatra*, *Pericles*, and *Coriolanus*. These three plays provided much inspiration for Eliot's poetry: *Antony and Cleopatra* for the second part of *The Waste Land*, *Coriolanus* for the unfinished play *Coriolan*, and *Pericles* for the poem *Marina*, the poet's first glimpse of Paradise. *Marina* concluded with a father's ecstatic reunion with his daughter, and *The Elder Statesman* ends on a similar note. Monica's compassion helps to facilitate her father's achievement of final peace, and Monica herself finds love with Charles. In real life, Eliot was both Lord Claverton and Charles. In his final act, with Valerie's help, he found both love and peace.

In 1959, Eliot told interviewer Donald Hall that, with *The Elder Statesman*, he had not quite reached the point he was aiming at, but he conceded, "I don't think I ever will."[54] By 1962, the poet had resigned himself to the idea that he would not produce any more poetry. Joseph Chiari reported that Eliot "would have very much liked to write a sixth play," but knew that he didn't have the physical or mental energy—a reality he accepted "without complaint."[5] Stephen Spender later opined that Eliot's last play did not quite "round off his lifework," but he went on to suggest that Eliot's final years with Valerie served as a natural and appropriate culmination of the poet's spiritual journey–concluding "with a return to human affection, acceptance of sensual experience and perhaps even a less catastrophic attitude towards society."[56]

Eliot himself clearly stated that, for him, the marriage superseded everything that had come before it. In 1960 he wrote, "Without the satisfaction of this happy marriage, no achievement or honour could give me satisfaction at all."[57] In the decades following her husband's death, Valerie Eliot offered a few intimate accounts of the simple happiness of their final years together. In 1994 she said, "He was made for marriage, he was a natural for it, a loving creature, and great fun, too. We used to stay at home and drink Drambuie and eat cheese and play Scrabble. He loved to win at cards, and I always made a point of losing by the time we went to bed."[58] Valerie was at her husband's side on the morning of January 4, 1965, when he died peacefully in their home of emphysema. The last word the poet spoke was his wife's name.

Valerie lived until 2012, long enough to become a devoted and inspirational guardian of her husband's work and legacy.

6. Eliot's Legacy

In the fall of 2008, Eliot scholar David Chinitz inaugurated a long-running column in *Time Present*, the American T. S. Eliot Society's triannual newsletter. That column, "Public Sightings," has catalogued Eliot allusions that Chinitz and others have found throughout 21st century's popular culture. Sightings began with a pair of Chicago newspaper articles lamenting the end of baseball season. "April is the cruelest month," one commentator wrote, while another intoned, "This is the way the season ends, not with a bang but a whimper." These phrases and others have become so ubiquitous that even the satirical TV series *The Simpsons* is in on the trend. In an episode of that long-running animated show, a roadie doing a mic check for a poetry reading (at Moe's Café Kafka) deadpans, "Roses are red. April is the cruelest month. *Cruelest month.*"

In 2010, *Slate* writer Chris Wilson opined that Eliot references seemed to be on the decline, but Chinitz has offered ample evidence to the contrary–and he has barely skimmed the surface. For every catalogued "public sighting," there are dozens more to be found. In addition to making regular appearances in crossword puzzles in *The New York Times Magazine* and *The* (London) *Times Literary Supplement*, as well as the occasional *Jeopardy!* episode, Eliot has inspired and influenced novels, TV shows, movies, songs, music albums, band names, comic books, video games, and more than a few political pundits.

The trend of basing book titles on Eliot's work began in the mid-20th century, with Evelyn Waugh's *A Handful of Dust*, Doris Lessing's *The Grass is Singing*, Nevil Shute's *On the Beach*, and Chinua Achebe's *No Longer at Ease*. Later, crime and mystery writers adopted Eliot as their poet laureate–an apt choice, since he loved crime and mystery novels. In Raymond Chandler's *The Long Goodbye*, private dick Philip Marlowe discusses the meaning of "The

Love Song of J. Alfred Prufrock" with a well-educated chauffer; both men admire the poet but conclude that he "didn't know very much about women." Lawrence Block borrowed the title of his crime novel *Time to Murder and Create* from Prufrock, while Brian Garfield paid homage to *The Waste Land* with the title *Fear in a Handful of Dust*. English mystery writer P. D. James acknowledged Eliot's poem "Whispers of Immortality" with her title *The Skull Beneath the Skin*, and Scottish crime writer Val McDermid paid tribute with several books in her Tony Hill / Carol Jordan series: *The Mermaids Singing*, *The Wire in the Blood* and *Fever of the Bone*. Martin Rowson's graphic novel *The Wasteland*, a mashup of Raymond Chandler and T. S. Eliot, has perhaps pulled off the biggest heist.

Young Adult novelists have a special affinity for Prufrock and his singing mermaids, who make cameos of one kind or another in Robert Cormier's *The Chocolate War*, Sarah Dessen's *Dreamland*, and John Green's *The Fault in Our Stars*. Prufrock has a prep school named after him in Lemony Snicket's *The Austere Academy*, and *The Waste Land* plays a crucial role in one of the other books in Snicket's *A Series of Unfortunate Events* series.

Science fiction and horror novelists gravitate toward the more enigmatic and ominous passages in *The Waste Land* and *The Hollow Men*. Fragments of those poems appear in *Swan Song* by Robert M. McCammon, *Consider Phlebas* and *Look to Windward* by Iain M. Banks, *Last Call* by Tim Powers, *The Eternal Footman* by James K. Morrow, *The Taking* by Dean R. Koontz, and throughout the work of Stephen King. Thomas Harris seems to be most impressed with Eliot's *Ash-Wednesday*; the heroine of his novel *The Silence of the Lambs* paraphrases a passage from that poem as a personal mantra.

Romance writers don't seem to take as much inspiration from Eliot's poetry, but the mock-romantic title "The Love Song of J. Alfred Prufrock" has proven ripe for parody. Some examples include Kinky Friedman's comedic novel *The Love Song of J. Edgar Hoover*, Carson Kreitzer's philosophical play *The Love Song of J. Robert Oppenheimer*, Teddy Wayne's young adult novel *The Love Song of Johnny Valentine*, and Rachel Joyce's picaresque *The Love Song of*

Miss Queenie Hennessey (whose title character measures out her life in ladies' shoes). Eliot's alleged affair with Emily Hale provides the backdrop for Martha Cooley's romance novel *The Archivist*, as well as a trilogy of romance books by Australian writer Steven Carroll (*The Lost Life*, *A World of Other People*, and *A New England Affair*). Carroll has also written a novel entitled *The Love Song of Lucy McBride*, so it is safe to assume that he's a fan. Eliot himself has the lead role—under the pseudonym Thomas Stern—in Kevin Davey's 2017 novel *Playing Possum*.

The poet's influence extends well beyond the print medium, into television and film. In recent years, Eliot has been quoted in the AMC series *Mad Men*, Showtime's *Dexter*, HBO's *Boardwalk Empire*, CBS's *The Good Wife* and *The Big Bang Theory*, History Channel's *Vikings*, A&E's *Bates Motel*, and NBC's *The Blacklist*, among others. On the silver screen, his poetry has been recited by Marlon Brando in *Apocalypse Now Redux*, Guy Pearce and Helena Bonham Carter in *Till Human Voices Wake Us*, Christopher Walken in *A Late Quartet*, and Sam Shepherd in *August: Osage County*. In 2014, "The Love Song of J. Alfred Prufrock" set the tone for one of the creepiest scenes in the indie horror film *It Follows*.

Director Christopher Nolan has cited *Four Quartets* as a major inspiration for his 2014 science fiction film *Interstellar*. Director Joss Whedon named a villainous army of robots after Eliot's "hollow men" in Marvel's *Avengers: Age of Ultron*. And comedian Seth Rogan quoted an intensely somber line from "Gerontion" in his raunchy sex comedy *Sausage Party*: "After such knowledge, what forgiveness?"

Indeed.

Eliot's legacy looms larger still over musicians. If one were going to make a mixtape of songs that reference the poet and/or his work—and what better way to pay homage to the allusive method?—one could include tunes by Bob Dylan ("Desolation Row"), Grateful Dead ("Dark Star"), Genesis ("The Cinema Show"), The Police ("Bring on the Night"), Crash Test Dummies ("Afternoons and Coffeespoons"), Arcade Fire ("We Used to Wait"), and countless others. Folk singer Frank Turner has a song entitled "I Knew

Prufrock Before He Got Famous," and comedian Bo Burnham sarcastically pays homage to Eliot's "traditional" love song in "Repeat Stuff." "The hollow men" is a popular catchphrase among death metal enthusiasts, along with "a handful of dust." Andrew Lloyd Webber has gone so far as to credit Eliot with the invention of rap, citing the lyrics to the cat poem "Rum Tum Tugger" as proof–although Chuck D's track "Niggativity ... Do I Dare Disturb the Universe?" might have been more of a mic drop.

Gamers have found allusions to Eliot's work in *Metal Gear Solid 2: Sons of Liberty*, *Halo 3*, and *Uncharted 3: Drake's Deception*, as well as an 8-bit online game called *The Waste Land: Eliot's Quest*. One likes to imagine academic source-hunters having a bit of fun with all of this, but no doubt they are also frustrated by the superficiality of most allusions. Do casual references ever draw new readers to serious contemplation of Eliot's poetry?

The poet's social criticism certainly continues to resonate within the Western world's political landscape. In 1960, a young U.S. Senator named John F. Kennedy quoted Eliot in a speech about the future of American society. Reflecting on a perceived cultural decline, he said, "I believe that we have followed too often [...] the words which T.S wrote in his poem [sic] *The Rock*," about a people whose "only monument" is "the asphalt road and a thousand lost golf balls." On the cusp of that pivotal decade in American culture, Kennedy insisted, "We can do better than that."

Twenty years later, a college student named Barack Obama privately mused that Eliot's work represents "a kind of conservativism which I respect more than bourgeois liberalism." This passage from the future president's college writings, uncovered by biographer David Maraniss in 2012, acknowledges the subtle nuances of Eliot's worldview and underscores the continued relevance of his social criticism.

In the 2003 documentary film *The Fog of War*, former U.S. Secretary of Defense Robert McNamara quotes a passage from "Little Gidding" as a correlative to his own experience of the ethos that produced the Vietnam War. "I'm not so naïve or simplistic to believe we're going to eliminate war," he noted. "We're not going to change human nature any time soon. It isn't that we aren't rational. We *are* rational. But reason has limits." Eliot tried to convey the same message during World War II, as nationalistic fervor threatened to destroy Western civilization. What would the poet think of our current political climate? Surely, his repeated warnings about "the awful daring of a moment's surrender / which an age of prudence can never retract" are relevant today. As he advised, we must approach the future with an awareness of the past, and constantly renew history so that we don't mindlessly repeat it.

Today, Eliot's poetry is usually remembered for its eerie imagery, and his critical writings for their rhetorical flair. Nuanced readings of his works (especially the later ones) mostly take place within academia. There is still, however, a wide variety of important voices echoing the poet's haunting cadences, dire prophecies, and ecstatic visions. In 1988, on the occasion of Eliot's 100th birthday, a symposium of contemporary American poets considered his elusive legacy in the pages of the *Southern Review*. Michael Ryan wrote about his own early experience of reading Eliot's work carnivorously, and about a younger generation that continues to digest the vitality of the elder statesman's words. Louise Glück remembered the terror of her initial discovery of Eliot, along with a feeling of instant connection, while Carol Muske-Dukes described a similar experience as proof that poetry can communicate before it is understood. Stephen Berg reflected on the subsequent search for greater understanding, and Donald Hall advised young readers to "return" to Eliot as a source for "everything necessary to the great tradition."

"If it isn't from Shakespeare or the Bible, it's from T. S. Eliot." So wrote Lisel Mueller, who insisted that Eliot is a "classic" because his poetic phrases have become an indelible part of our shared cultural lexicon—to say nothing of our collective unconscious. Although Eliot's celebrity persona has begun to recede into the historical background, his words endure, and his meanings still exist. Eliot continues to communicate with us; all we have to do is listen.

This is our beginning.

Endnotes

Preface

1. Eliot: *Complete Prose* V 569
2. Eliot: *Complete Prose* V 419
3. Eliot: *Letters* III 667
4. Eliot: *Complete Prose* I 769
5. Eliot: *To Criticize* 14
6. Eliot: *Complete Prose* IV 482

Chapter 1 – Prufrock and Other Observations

1. Eliot: *Christianity* 115
2. Hall: "T. S. Eliot"
3. Morley 128-129
4. quoted in "Mysterious"
5. Eliot: *Complete Poems* 465
6. Abigail Eliot quoted in "Mysterious"
7. Eliot: *To Criticize* 44
8. Levy 121
9. quoted in Gordon 209
10. Eliot: *On Poetry* 243
11. Sencourt 6
12. Eliot: *Letters* V 282
13. Eliot: *Complete Prose* III 492
14. Eliot: *Complete Prose* IV 688
15. Eliot: *Complete Prose* IV 591-592
16. T. S. Eliot quoted in Hall: "T. S. Eliot"
17. Eliot: *Complete Prose* IV 591
18. Eliot: *Complete Prose* I 10

19. Hall: "T. S. Eliot"
20. Chiari 12
21. quoted in Hall: *Remembering* 80
22. Aiken: *Clerk's*
23. Eliot: *Complete Prose* VI 759
24. Eliot: *Complete Prose* VI 514
25. Eliot: *Letters* V 35
26. Aiken: *Ushant* 143
27. Eliot: *Complete Prose* VI 514
28. Eliot: *Complete Prose* V 80
29. Eliot: *Complete Prose* V 81
30. quoted in Hargrove 41
31. Eliot: "Rhapsody" 15-16
32. Philippe 3
33. Philippe 9
34. Eliot: "Love" 130
35. Aiken: *Selected* 26
36. Aiken: *Ushant* 231
37. Aiken: *Selected* 29
38. Eliot: *Complete Prose* V 32
39. Eliot: *Complete Prose* II 449, 540
40. Eliot: *Complete Prose* V 646
41. Eliot: *Letters* I 88
42. Spender: *T. S. Eliot* 28
43. Pound: *Letters* 40
44. Eliot: *Letters* I 63
45. Eliot: *Letters* I 82

Chapter 2 – The Waste Land

1. Eliot: *Letters* I xix
2. Eliot: *Letters* I 118
3. Eliot: *Letters* I xix

4. Patmore 45
5. Patmore 85
6. quoted in Pearson 238
7. quoted in Pearson 238
8. Huxley 53
9. Sencourt 55
10. Russell: *Autobiography* 278
11. quoted in Monk 440
12. quoted in Seymour-Jones 97
13. quoted in Monk 440
14. Seymour-Jones 126
15. quoted in Monk 441
16. Russell: *Selected II* 129
17. quoted in Pearson 237-238
18. Eliot: *Letters* VI 562
19. Eliot: *Letters* I xix
20. Huxley 38
21. Tytell 119
22. Eliot: *To Criticize* 101
23. Huxley 46
24. quoted in Ackroyd 78
25. quoted in "Mysterious"
26. Eliot: *Letters* I 189, 210
27. Eliot: *Complete Prose* I 741
28. Eliot: *To Criticize* 52
29. Woolf: *Diary* II 67-68
30. Eliot: *Complete Prose* IV 770
31. Woolf: *Diary* II 68
32. Eliot: *Letters* I 386
33. Eliot: *Complete Prose* I 471-472
34. Eliot: *Letters* I 220
35. Eliot: "Tradition" 47
36. Eliot: *Letters* IV 573
37. Eliot: "Hamlet" 92
38. Eliot: "Hamlet" 91

39. Eliot: "Swinburne" 20
40. Eliot: *Complete Prose II* 380-381
41. Woolf: *Diary II* 189
42. Eliot: *Complete Prose II* 479
43. Woolf: *Diary II* 68
44. Eliot: *Letters I* 585
45. Eliot: *Waste* 32-33
46. Eliot: *Letters I* 603
47. Woolf: *Diary* IV 288
48. Eliot: *Complete Prose* IV 340
49. Eliot: *Complete Prose* IV 686
50. Pound: *Letters* 180
51. Woolf: *Diary II* 178
52. quoted in Brooker: *T.S. Eliot* 99
53. Eliot: *Letters* V 484
54. Hall: "T. S. Eliot"
55. Eliot: "Swinburne" 20
56. Eliot: *Letters* V 732
57. Eliot: *On Poetry* 122
58. Eliot: *Complete Prose* IV 840
59. Eliot: *Letters I* 786-787
60. Eliot: *Letters II* 11
61. Eliot: *Letters II* 76
62. Eliot: *Letters II* 124

Chapter 3 – Ash-Wednesday

1. Eliot: *Complete Prose* VI 713
2. Eliot: *Complete Prose II* 446
3. Hall: "T. S. Eliot"
4. quoted in Litz 10
5. Eliot: *Letters II* 268
6. Eliot: *Complete Prose* IV 712

7. Eliot: *Complete Prose II* 552-553
8. Eliot: "Eeldrop" 9
9. Valerie Eliot quoted in "Mysterious"
10. Eliot: *Complete Prose II* 555
11. Eliot: "Dante" 152
12. Eliot: *Complete Prose II* 555
13. Eliot: *Poems I* 714
14. Eliot: *Complete Prose IV* 157
15. Eliot: *Complete Prose III* 513
16. quoted in Brooker: *T. S. Eliot* 164
17. Woolf: *Letters III* 458
18. Woolf: *Letters III* 38
19. Eliot: *Letters I* 180
20. Eliot: *Letters II* 206
21. Eliot: *Complete Prose II* 461
22. Eliot: *Complete Prose II* 462
23. Eliot: *Letters II* 592
24. Eliot: *Letters II* 711
25. Eliot: *Letters II* 631
26. Eliot: *Letters III* 228
27. Eliot: *Letters VI* 291
28. Eliot: *Letters IV* 432
29. Pascal 73
30. Eliot: *Letters III* 428
31. Eliot: *Letters III* 209
32. Eliot: *Letters III* 255
33. Sencourt 124
34. Sencourt 125, 129
35. Eliot: *Letters III* 359 note 1
36. Eliot: *Complete Prose III* 48
37. Lehmann
38. Eliot: *Letters III* 700
39. Eliot: *Letters III* 861
40. Eliot: *Poems I* 759
41. Eliot: *Letters IV* 85

42. Eliot: *Complete Prose* V 472
43. Sencourt 134
44. Eliot: *Letters* IV 567
45. Eliot: *Letters* III 712-713
46. Eliot: *Complete Prose* II 822
47. Eliot: *Poems* I 94
48. Eliot: *Complete Prose* III 253
49. Eliot: *Complete Prose* III 704
50. Eliot: *Complete Prose* III 382
51. Eliot: *Letters* VII 618
52. Eliot: *Letters* V 258
53. Eliot: *Letters* V 179
54. Eliot: *Complete Prose* IV 704
55. Eliot: *Complete Prose* IV 161
56. Eliot: *Complete Prose* IV 161
57. Eliot: *Letters* V 270

Chapter 4 – Four Quartets

1. Eliot: *Complete Prose* IV 465
2. Gordon 241
3. Eliot: *Complete Prose* IV 240-241
4. Eliot: *Complete Prose* V 31
5. Eliot: *Complete Prose* V 43 note 54
6. Eliot: *Complete Prose* V 20
7. Eliot: *Complete Prose* III 535
8. Eliot: *Letters* I 550
9. Eliot: *To Criticize* 86
10. Eliot: *Complete Prose* VI 630
11. quoted in Schuchard: "Burbank" 17
12. quoted in Schuchard: "Burbank" 17
13. Eliot: *Letters* VI 286 note 2
14. quoted in Brinnin 287

15. Tomlin 21
16. Eliot: *Letters* VII 245 note 1
17. Hall: *Remembering* 109
18. Spender: *T. S. Eliot* 135
19. Eliot: *Letters* VI 584
20. Eliot: *Complete Prose* IV 821
21. Morley 126, 129
22. Eliot: *On Poetry* 99
23. Eliot: *Letters* I 243
24. Browne 9
25. Eliot: *Complete Prose* V 89
26. Eliot: *Complete Prose* V 398
27. Dukes 114
28. Gordon 268-269
29. Eliot: *Complete Poems* 275
30. Lehmann
31. quoted in Brooker: *T. S. Eliot* 572
32. Eliot: *Letters* VII 781
33. Smith 221
34. Eliot: *Complete Prose* V 221
35. Eliot: *Complete Prose* IV 29
36. Eliot: *On Poetry* 96
37. Eliot: *On Poetry* 87
38. quoted in Browne 107
39. Eliot: *Letters* VI 489
40. Tomlin 90
41. Valerie Eliot quoted in Morrison
42. Eliot: *Complete Prose* V 717
43. Eliot: *Complete Prose* V 127, 705
44. Eliot: *Letters* V 529
45. Eliot: *Complete Prose* IV 848
46. Sullivan 217
47. Eliot: *Complete Prose* VI 314
48. Hall: "T. S. Eliot"
49. Eliot: *Complete Prose* VI 321

50. Eliot: *Poems I* 893
51. Eliot quoted in Gardner 18
52. Eliot: *Poems I* 925
53. Eliot: *Poems I* 189
54. Eliot: *Poems I* 892
55. quoted in Schuchard: *Eliot's* 37
56. Eliot quoted in Gardner 24
57. quoted in Gardner 70
58. Sullivan 68
59. Eliot: "Tradition" 46
60. Eliot: *Complete Prose VI* 711-712
61. Eliot: "Preface" to *Thoughts* 13
62. Eliot: *On Poetry* 264
63. Eliot: *Complete Prose IV* 643
64. Eliot: *George* 29
65. Eliot: *On Poetry* 264
66. Hewes 32
67. Levy 41

Chapter 5 – The Elder Statesman

1. Sencourt 182
2. Eliot: *Complete Prose VI* 744
3. Eliot: *Complete Prose VI* 98
4. Tomlin 146
5. Arnold viii
6. Eliot: *Complete Prose IV* 180
7. Eliot: *Christianity* 177
8. Eliot: *Christianity* 116-117
9. Eliot: *Complete Prose VI* 716-717
10. Eliot: *Christianity* 153
11. Eliot: *Complete Prose VI* 648
12. Mary Trevelyan quoted in Seymour-Jones 584

13. T. S. Eliot quoted in Seymour-Jones 581
14. quoted in Du Sautoy 82
15. Gordon 404
16. Mary Trevelyan quoted in Seymour-Jones 584
17. Emily Hale quoted in Gordon 406
18. quoted in Behr 63
19. Spender: *T. S. Eliot* 252
20. Eliot: "Banquet" 421
21. Simpson 173
22. Breit
23. Brinnin 259
24. Mary Trevelyan quoted in Seymour-Jones 584
25. quoted in Gordon 486
26. Browne 342
27. Lehmann
28. Eliot: *On Poetry* 92
29. Eliot quoted in Brooker: *T. S. Eliot* 548
30. Browne 176
31. quoted in Browne 173
32. quoted in Brooker: *T. S. Eliot* 530
33. Eliot: *Complete Poems* 411, 420
34. Eliot: *On Poetry* 107
35. Eliot: *On Poetry* 107
36. quoted in Levy 40
37. Eliot: *Complete Prose II* 17
38. Eliot: *Letters VII* 230
39. quoted in Levy 51
40. McCrum
41. quoted in Brinnin 274
42. Morrison
43. quoted in Matthews 149
44. quoted in Gordon 520
45. Tomlin 195, 202
46. Chiari 55
47. Hall: *Remembering* 98

48. Browne 311
49. Eliot: *Complete Poems* 583
50. Browne 317
51. Eliot: *Complete Prose III* 711
52. Eliot: *To Criticize* 23
53. Eliot: *On Poetry* 93
54. Hall: "T. S. Eliot"
55. Chiari 28
56. Spender: *The 30s* 211
57. quoted in Gordon 511
58. Morrison

Chapter 7 – Suggested Reading

1. Eliot: *Complete Prose* V 67-68
2. Hinckley
3. Hastings 21
4. Gordinier 74
5. Eliot: *Letters* I 94
6. Eliot: *Letters* V 732
7. quoted in Brooker: T. S. *Eliot* 555
8. Eliot: *Letters* V 220
9. Heaney 50
10. Pound: "For" 92

Sources

Ackroyd, Peter. T. S. *Eliot: A Life*. New York: Simon & Schuster, 1984.

Aiken, Conrad. *The Clerk's Journal: Being a Diary of a Queer Man–An Undergraduate Poem together with A Brief Memoir of Harvard, Dean Briggs and* T. S. Eliot. New York: Eakins, 1971.

Aiken, Conrad. *Selected Letters of Conrad Aiken*. Ed. Joseph Killorin. New Haven: Yale UP, 1978.

Aiken, Conrad. *Ushant*. New York: Oxford, 1971.

Arnold, Matthew. *Culture and Anarchy*. London: Smith, Elder and Co., 1869.

Behr, Caroline. T. S. *Eliot: A Chronology of His Life and Works*. Salisbury: Macmillan, 1983.

Bennett, Arnold. *The Journal of Arnold Bennett*. New York: Literary Guild, 1933.

Breit, Harvey. "An Interview with T. S. Eliot–and Excerpts from His Birthday Book." *The New York Times*. November 21, 1948.

Brinnin, John Malcolm. *Sextet:* T. S. *Eliot & Truman Capote & Others*. New York: Delacorte, 1981.

Brooker, Jewel Spears, ed. T. S. *Eliot: The Contemporary Reviews*. Cambridge: Cambridge UP, 2004.

Browne, E. Martin. *The Making of* T. S. *Eliot's Plays*. New York: Cambridge UP, 1969.

Chiari, Joseph. T. S. *Eliot: A Memoir*. London: Enitharmon, 1982.

Du Sautoy, Peter. "T. S. Eliot: Personal Reminiscences." T. S. *Eliot: Essays from the Southern Review*. Ed. James Olney. Oxford: Oxford UP, 1988.

Dukes, Ashley. "T. S. Eliot in the Theatre." T. S. *Eliot: A Symposium*. Ed. Richard March and Tambimuttu. London: PL, 1948.

Eliot, T. S. "Banquet Speech." *Dictionary of Literary Biography* 329: *Nobel Prize Laureates in Literature*. Ed. Bruccoli Clark. Commerce: Cengage Gale, 2006.

Eliot, T. S. *Christianity and Culture: The Idea of a Christian Society and Notes towards the Definition of Culture*. New York: Harcourt, 1949.

Eliot, T. S. *The Complete Poems & Plays*. London: Faber, 1969.

Eliot, T. S. *The Complete Prose of T. S. Eliot: The Critical Edition, Volume 1: Apprentice Years, 1905-1918*. Ed. Jewel Spears Brooker and Ronald Schuchard. Baltimore: Johns Hopkins and Faber, 2014. Via Project Muse Online.

Eliot, T. S. *The Complete Prose of T. S. Eliot: The Critical Edition Volume 2: The Perfect Critic, 1919-1926*. Ed. Anthony Cuda and Ronald Schuchard. Baltimore: Johns Hopkins and Faber, 2014. Via Project Muse Online.

Eliot, T. S. *The Complete Prose of T. S. Eliot: The Critical Edition Volume 3: Literature, Politics, Belief 1927-1929*. Ed. Frances Dickey, Jennifer Formichelli and Ronald Schuchard. Baltimore: Johns Hopkins and Faber, 2015. Via Project Muse Online.

Eliot, T. S. *The Complete Prose of T. S. Eliot: The Critical Edition Volume 4: English Lion, 1930-1933*. Ed. Jason Harding and Ronald Schuchard. Baltimore: Johns Hopkins and Faber, 2015. Via Project Muse Online.

Eliot, T. S. *The Complete Prose of T. S. Eliot: The Critical Edition Volume 5: Tradition and Orthodoxy 1934–1939*. Ed. Iman Javadi, Ronald Schuchard and Jayme Stayer. Baltimore: Johns Hopkins and Faber, 2017. Via Project Muse Online.

Eliot, T. S. *The Complete Prose of T. S. Eliot: The Critical Edition Volume 6: The War Years, 1940-1946*. Ed. David E. Chinitz and Ronald Schuchard. Baltimore: Johns Hopkins and Faber, 2017. Via Project Muse Online.

Eliot, T. S. "Dante." *The Sacred Wood*. New York: Knopf, 1921.

Eliot, T. S. "Eeldrop and Appleplex." *The Little Review*. Ed. Margaret C. Anderson. May 1917.

Eliot, T. S. *George Herbert*. Plymouth: Northcote, 1962.

Eliot, T. S. "Hamlet." *The Sacred Wood*. New York: Knopf, 1921.

Eliot, T. S. *The Letters of T. S. Eliot Volume 1: 1898-1922 Revised Edition*. Ed. Valerie Eliot and Hugh Haughton. New Haven: Yale UP, 2009.

Eliot, T. S. *The Letters of T. S. Eliot Volume 2: 1923-1925*. Ed. Valerie Eliot and Hugh Haughton. London: Faber, 2009.

Eliot, T. S. *The Letters of T. S. Eliot Volume 3: 1926-1927*. Ed. Valerie Eliot and John Haffenden. London: Faber, 2012.

Eliot, T. S. *The Letters of T. S. Eliot Volume 4: 1928-1929*. Ed. Valerie Eliot and John Haffenden. London: Faber, 2013.

Eliot, T. S. *The Letters of T. S. Eliot Volume 5: 1930-1931*. Ed. Valerie Eliot and John Haffenden. London: Faber, 2014.

Eliot, T. S. *The Letters of T. S. Eliot Volume 6: 1932-1933*. Ed. Valerie Eliot and John Haffenden. London: Faber, 2016.

Eliot, T. S. *The Letters of T. S. Eliot Volume 7: 1934-1935*. Ed. Valerie Eliot and John Haffenden. London: Faber, 2017.

Eliot, T. S. "The Love Song of J. Alfred Prufrock." *Poetry: A Magazine of Verse*. Ed. Harriet Monroe. Vol. VI, No. III. June 1915.

Eliot, T. S. *On Poetry and Poets*. New York: Farrar, 1957.

Eliot, T. S. "Philip Massinger." *The Sacred Wood*. New York: Knopf, 1921.

Eliot, T. S. *The Poems of T. S. Eliot, Volume 1: Collected & Uncollected Poems*. Ed. Christopher Ricks and Jim McCue. Baltimore: Johns Hopkins, 2015.

Eliot, T. S. "Preface." *Thoughts for Meditation: A Way to Recovery from Within*. Ed. N. Gangulee. London: Faber, 1951.

Eliot, T. S. "Rhapsody on a Windy Night." *Others: An Anthology of the New Verse*. Ed. Alfred Kreymborg. New York: Knopf, 1917.

Eliot, T. S. "Swinburne as Critic." *The Sacred Wood*. New York: Knopf, 1921.

Eliot, T.S. *To Criticize the Critic and Other Writings*. Lincoln: U of Nebraska P, 1965.

Eliot, T. S. "Tradition and the Individual Talent." *The Sacred Wood*. New York: Knopf, 1921.

Eliot, T. S. *The Waste Land*. New York: Boni and Liveright, 1922.

Gardner, Helen. *The Composition of Four Quartets*. New York: Oxford, 1978.

Gordinier, Jeff. *X Saves the World: How Generation X Got the Shaft but Can Still Keep Everything From Sucking*. New York: Viking, 2008.

Gordon, Lyndall. *The Imperfect Life of T. S. Eliot*. London: Virago, 2012.

Hall, Donald. *Remembering Poets: Reminiscences and Opinions*. New York: Harper, 1978.

Hall, Donald. "T. S. Eliot, The Art of Poetry No. 1." *The Paris Review*, No. 21, Spring-Summer 1959.

Hargrove, Nancy. *T. S. Eliot's Parisian Year*. Gainesville: UP of Florida, 2009.

Hastings, Michael. *Tom & Viv*. New York: Penguin, 1984.

Heaney, Seamus. *Finders Keepers: Selected Prose 1971-2001*. New York: Farrar, 2002.

Hewes, Henry. "T. S. Eliot at Seventy." *The Saturday Review*. September 13, 1958.

Hinckley, David. "T. S. Eliot really liked cats–according to his wife." *New York Daily News*. 8 October 1982.

Huxley, Aldous. *Selected Letters of Aldous Huxley*. Ed. James Sexton. Chicago: Ivan R. Dee, 2007.

Lehmann, John. "T. S. Eliot Talks About Himself and the Drive to Create." *The New York Times*. November 9, 1953.

Levy, William Turner and Victor Scherle. *Affectionately, T. S. Eliot: The Story of a Friendship: 1947-1965*. Philadelphia: Lippincott, 1968.

Litz, A. Walton. "Introduction and Afterword." *T. S. Eliot: Essays from the Southern Review*. Ed. James Olney. Oxford: Clarendon, 1988.

Matthews, T. S. *Great Tom: Notes Towards the Definition of T. S. Eliot*. New York: Harper, 1974.

McCrum, Robert. "Revealed: the remarkable tale of T. S. Eliot's late love affair." *The Observer*. 23 March 2009.

Monk, Ray. *Bertrand Russell: The Spirit of Solitude, 1872-1921*. New York: Free Press, 1996.

Morley, Frank. "A Few Recollections of Eliot." *The Sewanee Review*, Vol. 74, No. 1, Winter 1966.

Morrison, Frank. "The Two Mrs. Eliots." *The Independent*, 24 April 1994.

"The Mysterious Mr. Eliot." *Omnibus*, Season 5, Episode 1, BBC, 3 January 1971.

Pascal, Blaise. *The Harvard Classics, Volume 48: Blaise Pascal–Thoughts, Letters and Minor Works*. Trans. W.F. Trotter. New York: Collier, 1910.

Patmore, Brigit. *My Friends When Young: The Memoirs of Brigit Patmore*. London: Heinemann, 1968.

Pearson, John. *The Sitwells: A Family's Biography*. New York: Harcourt, 1978.

Philippe, Charles-Louis. *Bubu of Montparnasse*. Trans. Laurence Vail. London: Weidenfeld, 1952.

Pound, Ezra. "For T.S.E." *T. S. Eliot: The Man and His Work*. Ed. Allen Tate. Sewanee: The University of the South, 1966.

Pound, Ezra. *The Letters of Ezra Pound*, 1907-1941. Ed. D.D. Paige. New York: Harvest, 1950.

Russell, Bertrand. *The Autobiography of Bertrand Russell* 1914-1944. New York: Simon & Schuster, 1969.

Russell, Bertrand. *The Selected Letters of Bertrand Russell, Volume 2: The Public Years* 1914-1970. Ed. Nicholas Griffin. London: Routledge, 2002.

Schuchard, Ronald. "Burbank with a Baedeker, Eliot with a Cigar." *Modernism/Modernity*, January 2003.

Schuchard, Ronald. *Eliot's Dark Angel: Intersections of Life and Art*. New York: Oxford, 1999.

Sencourt, Robert. *T. S. Eliot: A Memoir*. Ed. Donald Adamson. New York: Dodd, 1971.

Seymour-Jones, Carole. *Painted Shadow: The Life of Vivienne Eliot, First Wife of T. S. Eliot, and the Long-Suppressed Truth About Her Influence on His Genius*. New York: Doubleday, 2001.

Simpson, Eileen. *Poets in Their Youth: A Memoir*. New York: Farrar, 1982.

Smith, Janet Adam. "Tom Possum and the Roberts Family." *T. S. Eliot: Essays from the Southern Review*. Ed. James Olney. Oxford: Clarendon, 1988.

Spender, Stephen. *The 30s and After: Poetry, Politics, People,* 1930s-1970s. New York: Random House, 1978.

Spender, Stephen. *T. S. Eliot*. New York: Viking, 1976.

Sullivan, J. W. N. *Beethoven: His Spiritual Development*. New York: Knopf, 1947.

Tomlin, E. W. F. *T. S. Eliot: A Friendship*. London: Routledge, 1988.

Tytell, John. *Ezra Pound: The Solitary Volcano*. New York: Anchor, 1988.

Woolf, Virginia. *The Diary of Virginia Woolf Volume Two: 1920-1924*. Ed. Anne Olivier Bell. New York: Harcourt, 1978.

Woolf, Virginia. *The Diary of Virginia Woolf Volume Four: 1931-1935*. Ed. Anne Oliver Bell. New York: Harcourt, 1982.

Woolf, Virginia. *The Letters of Virginia Woolf Volume Three: 1923-1928*. Ed. Nigel Nicolson and Joanne Trautmann. Boston: Harvest, 1977.

Suggested Reading

For half a century after his death, T. S. Eliot's literary work existed in a state of fragmentation. For future readers that will not be the case. In 2015, Faber & Faber and the Johns Hopkins University Press jointly published *The Poems of T. S. Eliot* in two volumes, edited and thoroughly annotated by Christopher Ricks and Jim McCue. These two volumes contain all of Eliot's extant verse poetry, along with expert commentary and textual histories. Beginning in 2014, the two publishers also began releasing eight volumes of *The Complete Prose of T. S. Eliot* in digital format. Collected and annotated under the general editorship of Ronald Schuchard, these volumes replace all the prose collections that were published during Eliot's lifetime and incorporate a wealth of previously uncollected essays, reviews, introductions, and unpublished material. A scholarly edition of *The Complete Plays of T. S. Eliot* has been announced, and will be edited by John Haffenden. In the meantime, Haffenden is preoccupied with his role as editor of *The Letters of T. S. Eliot*. In 2020, the Emily Hale correspondence housed at Princeton University will also become available to researchers.

In addition to these primary sources, Eliot scholars and enthusiasts can consult a wide range of secondary sources for insights into the poet and his work. Firsthand accounts of Eliot's life can be found in the letters, memoirs, and biographies of many of his contemporaries, including Conrad Aiken, Richard Aldington, Aldous Huxley, Wyndham Lewis, John Malcolm Brinnin, Ottoline Morrell, John Middleton Murry, Brigit Patmore, Ezra Pound, Bertrand Russell, Osbert Sitwell, Stephen Spender, Leonard Woolf, and Virginia Woolf. Some of these figures contributed essays to one or more literary tributes to Eliot, including *T. S. Eliot: A Symposium* (1949), edited by Richard March and Tambimuttu; *T. S. Eliot: A Symposium for His 70th Birthday* (1958), edited by Neville

Braybrooke; *T. S. Eliot: The Man and His Work* (1966), edited by Allen Tate; and *T. S. Eliot: Essays from the Southern Review* (1988), edited by James Olney. Also worthwhile is a 1971 episode of the BBC TV series *Omnibus* entitled "The Mysterious Mr. Eliot," which features rare interviews with friends and family members, including first cousins Abigail Eliot and Eleanor Hinkley, sister-in-law Theresa Eliot, friend Hope Mirlees, and wife Valerie Eliot. Five of Eliot's peers have published book-length memoirs about their relationships with the poet, and these are also worth reading for additional (if biased) context: *Affectionately, T. S. Eliot* (1968) by William Turner Levy; *The Making of T. S. Eliot's Plays* (1969) by E. Martin Browne; *T. S. Eliot: A Memoir* (1971) by Robert Sencourt; *T. S. Eliot: A Memoir* (1982) by Joseph Chiari; and *T. S. Eliot: A Friendship* (2000) by E. W. F. Tomlin. Mary Trevelyan's memoir *The Pope of Russell Square* (written in the late 1950s) remains unpublished, but hopefully not for much longer.

With so much research material available, it is not surprising that there have been many written biographies about the famous poet. The first full biography was T. S. Matthews' meandering *Great Tom* (1973), followed by Peter Ackroyd's more traditional *T. S. Eliot* (1984). In 1983, Ronald Bush wrote a compelling psychological biography, *T. S. Eliot: A Study in Character and Style*, which is especially valuable for its insights into the poetry of Eliot's middle years. Lyndall Gordon was the first author to attempt a major critical biography. Her book *The Imperfect Life of T. S. Eliot* (1998, revised 2012) presents Eliot's work within the context of a spiritual autobiography. Gordon's work has been followed by two comparatively concise biographies: Craig Raine's entry in Oxford University Press's *Lives and Legacies* series (2006) and John Worthen's *T. S. Eliot: A Short Biography* (2011). Most recently, Scottish poet Robert Crawford has undertaken a massive two-volume biography aimed at humanizing Eliot while avoiding long-held assumptions about his life and work. The first volume, *Young Eliot: From St. Louis to The Waste Land*, was published in 2015.

The vast body of secondary critical works about Eliot is much more intimidating–reminding one of Eliot's comment that "the student of Shakespeare may well wonder whether he should consume his time over Shakespeare criticism at all." In the 1934 essay "Shakespearean Criticism," Eliot concluded that an awareness of "the whole pattern formed by Shakespeare criticism from his time to ours" is necessary for a true understanding of the greatness of the poet.[1] He then helpfully offered a concise overview of Shakespeare criticism.

In the 1994 edition of *The Cambridge Companion to T. S. Eliot*, Eliot scholar Jewel Spears Brooker provided a similar overview of Eliot criticism, dividing the major works into three phases. Brooker wrote that during the first phase, beginning in the late 1920s and continuing through the 1950s, the major critics generally lauded Eliot as the leading poet of his time. Major works published during this period include the writings of I. A. Richards (*Principles of Literary Criticism*), Edmund Wilson (*Axel's Castle*), F. R. Leavis (*New Bearings in English Poetry*), R. P. Blackmur (*The Double Agent*), Cleanth Brooks (*Modern Poetry and the Tradition*), and Frank Kermode (*The Romantic Image*). Among those who wrote entire books about Eliot, the most reputable are F. O. Matthiessen (*The Achievement of T. S. Eliot*), Helen Gardner (*The Art of T. S. Eliot*), Kristian Smidt (*Poetry and Belief in the Work of T. S. Eliot*), Grover Smith (*T. S. Eliot's Poetry and Plays: A Study in Sources and Meanings*), Hugh Kenner (*T. S. Eliot: The Invisible Poet*) and Herbert Howarth (*Notes on Some Figures Behind T. S. Eliot*). *T. S. Eliot: A Selected Critique*, edited by Leonard Unger, and *T. S. Eliot: The Contemporary Reviews*, edited by Jewel Spears Brooker, are judicious anthologies of critical responses to Eliot's work during this first phase.

In the later years of the poet's life, and throughout the two decades following his death, Eliot's reputation suffered a critical backlash. On a more positive note, however, a number of publications during this time suggested exciting new avenues of study. David E. Jones' *The Plays of T. S. Eliot* (1960) and Carol H. Smith's *T. S. Eliot Dramatic Theory and Practice* (1963) remain the most comprehensive studies of Eliot as dramatist. The 1964 publication of Eliot's doctoral dissertation, as *Knowledge and Experience in the Philosophy of F. H. Bradley*, encouraged studies of Eliot as a philosopher; *T. S. Eliot's Intellectual and Poetic Development* 1909-1922 by Piers Gray is a prime example. The 1967 publication of *The Criterion* in 18 volumes also prompted scholars to re-examine Eliot's social criticism and political thought. Two books published in 1971–*Eliot and His Age* by Russell Kirk, and *T. S. Eliot's Social Criticism* by Roger Kojecky–remain authoritative, and *T. S. Eliot's Intellectual Development* 1922-1939 by John D. Margolis offers a compelling overview of Eliot's philosophical writings. Also in 1971, Valerie Eliot's *The Waste Land: A Facsimile and Transcript* inaugurated a period of reevaluation of Eliot's early masterpiece, highlights of which include Anne Bolgan's *What the Thunder Really Said* (1973), and the anthologies *Eliot in His Time* (1973), edited by A. Walton Litz, and *The Waste Land in Different Voices* (1974), edited by A.D. Moody. Helen Gardner's book *The Composition of Four Quartets*, published in 1978, likewise renewed interest in Eliot's later masterpiece. Toward the end of this phase, Frank Kermode's *Selected Prose of* T. S. *Eliot* (1975) added a few neglected prose pieces to the relatively gaunt body of Eliot's collected literary criticism.

Esteem for T. S. Eliot's work rose and fell dramatically in the early 1980s, when the poet posthumously reached his biggest audience. In 1981, Andrew Lloyd Webber's musical *Cats*–based on Eliot's *Old Possum's Book of Practical Cats*–opened at The New London Theatre and became a runaway hit. Valerie Eliot, who authorized the adaptation, insisted that her husband would have been proud, because "he loved the Music Hall and this is the closest his work would have come to it."[2] *Cats* went on to become one of the longest-running musicals in Broadway history, and remains popular today.

In 1984, a critical backlash against T. S. Eliot peaked with the West End production of Michael Hastings' salacious play *Tom & Viv*. Hastings–who openly described his play as a work of fiction–depicted Eliot as a heartless fascist who colluded with Bertrand Russell to seduce and destroy his wife Vivienne, and later manipulated Vivienne's brother Maurice Haigh-Wood into having her committed to an insane asylum on false pretenses. According to Hastings, Maurice claimed that when he visited Vivienne there shortly before her death, he realized that "she was as sane as I was."[3] It is difficult to verify or refute any claim about Vivienne's mental state in the 1940s, but it is fair to conclude that most of *Tom & Viv* is... well.... fiction.

In 1988, Eliot scholars celebrated the poet's centennial birthday. Jewel Spears Brooker marks this as the beginning of the third and current phase in Eliot studies, during which critics generally have been more sympathetic to the poet and more understanding about the nuances of his thoughts and beliefs. This generation of critics has taken it upon themselves to preserve all of Eliot's work for posterity, and to safeguard his legacy against libelous criticism. Important early publications during this phase included *The Varieties of Metaphysical Poetry*, previously unpublished transcripts of Eliot's 1926 Clark Lectures and his 1932-33 lectures at Johns Hopkins University, as well as *Inventions of the March Hare*, Eliot's unpublished poetry and fragments written between 1909 to 1917. These works anticipated the comprehensive T. S. Eliot Editorial Project, which aims to bring all of Eliot's poems, plays, and prose back into print by the 2020s.

Major works of Eliot criticism in the intervening years have included *T. S. Eliot and Indic Traditions: A Study of Poetry and Belief* by Cleo McNelly Kearns; *T. S. Eliot and the Philosophy of Criticism* by Richard Schusterman; *T. S. Eliot and Prejudice* by Christopher Ricks; *The American T. S. Eliot: A Study of the Early Writings* by Eric Sigg; *Skepticism and Modern Enmity: Before and After Eliot* by Jeffrey M. Perl; *Reading "The Waste Land": Modernism and the Limits of Interpretation* by Jewel Spears Brooker and Joseph Bentley; *Mastery and Escape: T. S. Eliot and the Dialectic of Modernism* by Brooker; *T. S. Eliot, Anti-Semitism and Literary Form* by Anthony Julius; *T. S. Eliot and American Poetry* by Lee Oser; *A Critical Difference: T. S. Eliot and John Middleton Murry in English Literary Criticism 1919-1928* by David Goldie; *Eliot's Dark Angel: Intersections of Life and Art* by Ronald Schuchard; *From Philosophy to Poetry: T. S. Eliot's*

Study of Knowledge and Experience by Donald J. Childs; *T. S. Eliot and the Cultural Divide* by David E. Chinitz; *Redeeming Time: T. S. Eliot's "Four Quartets"* by Kenneth Paul Kramer; *Modernism, Memory and Desire: T. S. Eliot and Virginia Woolf* by Gabrielle McIntire; and *"Anglo-Catholic in Religion": T. S. Eliot and Christianity* by Barry Spurr, and many others. Also noteworthy are several wide-ranging scholarly collections: *The Cambridge Companion to T. S. Eliot*, edited by A. David Moody; *T. S. Eliot in Context*, edited by Jason Harding; *A Companion to T. S. Eliot*, edited by Chinitz; *The New Cambridge Companion to T. S. Eliot*, edited by Harding; and the *T. S. Eliot Studies Annual*, inaugurated in 2017 under the editorship of John D. Morgenstern.

Within a few years, all of Eliot's work will be available in scholarly editions, setting the stage for a new phase of Eliot criticism. Where will Eliot studies go from there? Conrad Aiken famously declared the 20th century "The Age of Eliot," and he was not alone in suggesting that Eliot largely furnished and defined the Modern Mind as we know it. What, then, will be the poet's place in the rapidly-accelerating Information Age of the 21st century? Will his work remain vital for rising generations or will it be relegated to history?

As an Eliot enthusiast, I can only offer biased speculations. I came to Eliot (via "The Love Song of J. Alfred Prufrock") as a member of America's so-called Generation X, the first generation to come of age with easy Internet access to help answer our overwhelming questions. Jeff Gordinier, author of the generational study *X Saves the World*, has referred to us as "a generation of Prufrocks, forever hesitating before making the leap."[4] Why the hesitation? Because we are overwhelmed by seemingly unlimited access to so much information and so many options. We have the world at our fingertips, and so we are overwhelmed by answers.

Some sociologists have speculated this new glut of immediately-accessible information will have an increasingly negative effect on future generations of all countries–slowly dulling intellectual curiosity, and contributing to a loss of critical thinking skills, illusions of comprehensive knowledge, and a general deterioration of our ability to focus, reflect and synthesize the overwhelming data of our lives. *Where is the life we have lost in living? Where is the wisdom we have lost in knowledge? Where is the knowledge we have lost in information?* These are the questions that Eliot posed in his 1934 play *The Rock*, and they obviously remain relevant today.

Throughout this collective body of work, the poet offered some suggestions for the future. His poetry illustrates how we can expand human consciousness by probing the frontiers of language. His literary criticism reveals methods for unlocking the transformative power that resides in poems and stories, philosophies and religions (both ancient and modern). His life illustrates a pattern of growth—marred by missteps, of course, because Eliot was no saint or mystic, but illuminating for those who can hear his voice. If his work speaks to you, there is much to discover.

In a 1915 letter to Ezra Pound, Eliot wrote that "the only kind of art worth talking about is the art one happens to like."[5] If a poem doesn't resonate with you, he suggested, then forget it; leave it for someone else to find. If it does speak to you, then begin your journey. For some readers, this means embarking on a process of intellectual analysis—but Eliot cautioned us not to forget our initial emotional response. In a 1931 letter to fellow literary critic I. A. Richards, he warned, "If the reader knows too much about the crude material in the author's mind, his own reaction may tend to become at best merely a kind of feeble image of the author's feelings, whereas a good poem should have a potentiality of evoking feelings and associations in the reader of which the author is wholly ignorant."[6] He echoed this sentiment in a 1949 interview about his most popular play, *The Cocktail Party*, saying, "Whatever the play's message is, it is as much a matter of what message the audience finds in it as what message I put in it, and if there is nothing more in the play than what I was aware of meaning, then it must be a pretty thin piece of work."[7] The meaning of a work of art, Eliot insisted, is always more than the creator's intentions, more than the audience's associations, more than any critic can hope to summarize. Ultimately, it is more than can ever be understood, in the most conventional sense of that word. "'Understanding' poetry," Eliot told theologian G. W. S. Curtis in 1930, "seems to me largely to consist of coming to see that it is not necessary to 'understand.'"[8]

This is not to say that one shouldn't study poetry, but that one must eventually surrender intellectual study and return to the poem for a renewed and deeper experience. The renowned Irish poet Seamus Heaney, winner of the 1995 Nobel Prize in Literature, put it this way:

> What is to be learned from Eliot is the double-edged nature of poetic reality: first encountered as a strange fact of culture, poetry is internalized over the years until it becomes, as they say, second nature. Poetry that was originally beyond you, generating the need to understand and overcome its strangeness, becomes in the end a familiar path within you, a grain along which your imagination opens pleasurably backwards towards an origin and a seclusion. Your last state is therefore a thousand times better than your first, for the experience of poetry is one which truly deepens and fortifies itself with reenactment.[9]

Surely that is a vital and important experience at any age. With that in mind, I can only repeat the short eulogy that Ezra Pound gave for his friend T. S. Eliot—and with the urgency of a young explorer seeing a new world for the first time. "READ HIM."[10]

About the Author

Joseph Maddrey is a freelance writer, TV producer and author of several books, including *The Making of T. S. Eliot: A Study of the Literary Influences* (2009).

A Word from the Publisher

Thank you for reading *Simply Eliot*!

If you enjoyed reading it, we would be grateful if you could help others discover and enjoy it too.

Please review it with your favorite book provider such as Amazon, BN, Kobo, Apple Books, or Goodreads, among others.

Again, thank you for your support and we look forward to offering you more great reads.

Printed in Great Britain
by Amazon